Violetta Dubinina, M.S

SHSAT
MATH
THE NEW
APPROACH

8 review lessons on most common SHSAT topics with 25 practice questions in each (200 practice questions total)

1 complete SHSAT Math Practice Test

Fully up-to-date for the current exam

January 2025 Edition

Table of Contents

Introduction

The structure of this book is based on extensive feedback from students who have been practicing for the Specialized High School Admission Test and have asked for a way to prepare for the mathematics portion of the exam by targeting specific topics and areas, rather than using complete practice tests that have a variety of problems.

Many students reported that a lot of their errors resulted not from being unable to solve any given problem, but rather from forgetting a specific definition (for example, the difference between whole and natural numbers) or a particular concept.

This book allows you to practice for the test by using a new approach: tackling and improving one area at a time. The book is organized into 8 mini-lessons which cover the most common types of problems that appear on the SHSAT exam. Each lesson reminds you of the definitions or principles for that topic that are most often forgotten, and also suggests further topics if you need a more extensive review. Included with each lesson are a few example problems that demonstrate the various facets of the covered topic, and 25 practice problems that allow you to take a deep dive and practice the specific techniques and methods rigorously.

The best way to use this book is to select an 8 week period, and concentrate on one lesson each week (if you are able to get through lessons quickly, you can also condense this time period – if a lesson only takes you a day to finish, there's no need to wait for a week to move on to the next one). Thoroughly review the concepts presented in the current lesson, and then work on the 25 practice problems, concentrating on speed and solving without errors. Remember that the actual test expects you to complete each question in about 1.5 minutes: therefore, it's best to aim to complete each set of 25 practice questions in about 35 minutes (accounting for distractions and time needed to check your work).

Be mindful of the methods, concepts, and definitions you are using when working on the problems. You will notice that topics also overlap a bit, and some of the ideas you've reviewed in previous lessons show up in subsequent ones.

Finally, once you've completed all 8 lessons and solved all 200 practice problems, take the full practice exam presented at the end of the book, again aiming for speed and correctness. You should be able to notice a considerable improvement in your command of the covered topics and in your ability to identify what area any given problem belongs to and what approach should be taken to solve it.

When you are finished with this book, continue practicing with complete SHSAT math exams (from the other two books in this series, shown on the back cover) to further improve your speed and accuracy.

Wishing you great success on the SHSAT exam,
Violetta Dubinina

SHSAT Lesson 1: Common Number Sets

In this lesson:

Definitions of common number sets: natural numbers, whole numbers, integers, even and odd numbers, prime and composite numbers.

Divisibility concepts: prime factorization, greatest common factor and least common multiple.

Terminology: Distinct numbers.

What you must know

Definitions

Natural numbers or counting numbers are 1, 2, 3, 4, 5, 6, and so on. Note that 0 is **not** included.

Whole numbers are 0, 1, 2, 3, 4, 5, and so on. Note that 0 is included.

Integers are all whole numbers and their opposites: ..., −3, −2, −1, 0, 1, 2, 3, ...

Prime numbers are **integers** that are greater than 1 and have exactly two factors, 1 and themselves. 2 is the only even prime number. Examples of other prime numbers include: 3, 5, 7, 11, 13, 17, 19, 23, 29, 31, 37, 41, 43, 53, 59, 61, 67, 71, ...

Composite numbers are **integers** that have **more** than two factors.

Distinct numbers simply means that the two numbers are **different** from each other.

Even numbers are integers that are divisible by 2. Even numbers can be negative.

Odd numbers are integers that are not divisible by 2. Odd numbers can be negative.

GCF (Greatest Common Factor) of two or more integers is the largest number that is the factor of each. For example, GCF(24,36,60) = 12.

LCM (Least Common Multiple) of two or more integers is the smallest integer that is divisible by each. For example, LCM(24,36,60) = 360.

Divisibility Rules

The following rules allow you to quickly check for divisibility by certain small integers.

Divisible by 2: The last digit of the integer must be even.

Divisible by 3: The sum of all digits of the integer must be divisible by 3.

Divisible by 4: The last 2 digits of the integer is a number that is divisible by 4 (12, 16, 20, 24, and so on).

Divisible by 5: The last digit of the integer must be 5 or 0.

Divisible by 6: The integer is divisible by 2 and by 3.

Divisible by 9: The sum of all digits of the integer must be divisible by 9.

Divisible by 10: The last digit of the integer must be 0.

Prime Factorization

There are two easy ways to split a number into prime factors. One way is to first split the number into two largest factors, and then keep splitting each factor into smaller factors, until all factors are prime. For example, to split 120 into prime factors, you would do the following:

$$
\begin{array}{c}
120 \\
12 \quad\quad 10 \\
2 \quad 6 \quad 2 \quad 5 \\
2 \quad 3
\end{array}
$$

Therefore, $120 = 2 \cdot 2 \cdot 2 \cdot 3 \cdot 5$ is the final prime factorization. It can also be expressed as $120 = 2^3 \cdot 3 \cdot 5$.

The second way of splitting a number into prime factors is by repeatedly dividing it by the smallest possible prime factor, until the result of the division is 1. For example:

Number	120	60	30	15	5	1
Factors	2	2	2	3	5	

Sample Problems

1. What is the difference between the LCM and the GCF of 40 and 48?

      A. 248   **B.** 240   **C.** 232   **D.** 128   **E.** 8

Solution

First, split the given numbers into prime factors, so you can identify the factors they have in common:

$$40 = 2 \cdot 2 \cdot 2 \cdot 5$$
$$48 = 2 \cdot 2 \cdot 2 \cdot 2 \cdot 3$$

The greatest common factor is the product of the prime factors that both numbers share. In this case, it is:

$$GCF = 2 \cdot 2 \cdot 2 = 8$$

Finally, the least common multiple is the smallest number divisible by both given numbers. Notice that 48 already contains all the factors of 40 except 5. Therefore, the least common multiple is:

$$LCM = 48 \cdot 5 = 240$$

The difference is $240 - 8 = 232$. Therefore, the answer is **C.**

2. Which number could not be the sum of two prime numbers?

      A. 53   **B.** 39   **C.** 33   **D.** 31   **E.** 19

Solution

The sum of two prime numbers is always an even number except in a case when **one of the primes is 2**. Since all the possible answers are odd, we can be certain that one of the two primes is 2. We can then express each answer as a sum of 2 and another number:

$$53 = 2 + 51, \ 39 = 2 + 37, \ 33 = 2 + 31, \ 31 = 2 + 29, \ 19 = 2 + 17$$

Each sum is a sum of two primes except for the first one, because 51 is not a prime ($51 = 3 \cdot 17$). Therefore, the answer is **A.**

Practice Problems

1. If $\frac{n}{9}$ is an integer, which of the following could be the value of n?

   A. 135
   B. 136
   C. 137
   D. 138

2. What is the sum of all distinct prime factors of 48?

   E. 11
   F. 7
   G. 6
   H. 5

3. The product of three consecutive numbers **cannot** be:

   A. 210
   B. 336
   C. 560
   D. 1716

4. Which of the following is a prime number between $50\frac{2}{3}$ and $57\frac{3}{4}$?

   E. 51
   F. 53
   G. 55
   H. 57

5. Which of the following sets of numbers consists of elements that are all either odd or prime numbers between 0 and 10?

   A. {1, 3, 5, 7, 9}
   B. {1, 2, 3, 5, 7, 9}
   C. {2, 3, 5, 7, 9}
   D. {1, 2, 3, 4, 5, 7, 9}

6. If $(b + 4)$ is an odd number, which of the following must also be odd?

   E. $b - 3$
   F. $b + 3b$
   G. $b + 1$
   H. $b - 2$

7. If y is an even number, what is the smallest odd number that is greater than $2y + 1$?

   A. $y + 1$
   B. $2y + 3$
   C. $2y + 1$
   D. 13

8. If P is a product of an odd prime number and an even integer, then P **cannot** be equal to:

   E. 16
   F. 14
   G. 10
   H. 6

9. The prime factorization of 72 is:

   A. $2^2 \cdot 3^2$
   B. $2^2 \cdot 3^3$
   C. $2^3 \cdot 3^2$
   D. $23 \cdot 32$

10. At a recording studio raffle, every 9th customer wins a CD, and every 12th customer wins a DVD. Which of the following customers will win both a CD and a DVD?

   E. 21st
   F. 24th
   G. 36th
   H. 48th

11. Which property makes the statement $4(12 - 7) = 48 - 28$ true?

   A. Commutative property
   B. Associative property
   C. Distributive property
   D. Identity property

12. What is the smallest possible average of three distinct positive even integers?

   E. 4
   F. 2
   G. 6
   H. None of these

13. $56 \div (-9 + 2)(3) - 10 + 3 \div (-1) + 38 =$

   A. 12
   B. 24
   C. −29
   D. 1

14. How many more integers from 1 to 200 (inclusive) are divisible by 11 than the number of integers in the same interval which are divisible by 3 and by 7?

   E. 12
   F. 11
   G. 10
   H. 9

15. My car is stuck in traffic. There are twice as many cars in front of my car than behind my car. How many cars are there in my line, if my car is 29th from the front?

   A. 14
   B. 28
   C. 43
   D. 56

16. Let x and y be integers. When dividing x by y, the remainder is zero. If $y = 2$, then x:

   E. Must be an even number
   F. Can be even or odd
   G. Must be an odd number
   H. Doesn't have known properties

17. If $a : b = 3 : 7$ and $b : c = 1 : 3$, what is $a : c$?

 A. $1 : 2$
 B. $1 : 3$
 C. $1 : 7$
 D. $2 : 3$

18. If $m + n = 11$ and $m - n = 3$, what is the value of $m^2 - n^2$?

 E. 33
 F. 31
 G. 27
 H. None of the above

19. All of the following numbers are factors of 120, **except**:

 A. 8
 B. 15
 C. 30
 D. 36

20. When written in a decimal form, which of these is a terminating decimal?

 E. 41/40
 F. 5/6
 G. 3/11
 H. 11/3

21. What is the difference between the LCM and the GCF of 42 and 12?

 A. 82
 B. 78
 C. 34
 D. 26

22. If P is the product of an odd prime number and an odd integer, P **cannot** be equal to:

 E. 21
 F. 55
 G. 33
 H. 6

23. What is the average of all multiples of 7 between 27 and 120?

 A. 57.5
 B. 59.5
 C. 63.5
 D. 73.5

24. What is the largest 3-digit integer that is divisible by 13?

 E. 975
 F. 997
 G. 988
 H. 1001

25. If 5 less than 3 times the integer is one-half of 26, what is the integer?

 A. 3
 B. 5
 C. 6
 D. 11

In this lesson:

Definitions of a pattern and a sequence: patterns of symbols and sequences of numbers.

Rules: Determining what comes next or what's missing in a pattern or sequence by figuring out what rules they follow.

Terminology: Mean (or average), median.

What you must know

Definitions

A pattern is a set of elements (numbers, symbols, or pictures) that are arranged following a particular rule. For example, consider the following pattern of numbers:

$$3, 10, 17, 24, 31, \ldots$$

This pattern follows this rule: "*start with 3, and add 7 for each subsequent element*". A pattern can also consist of non-numerical symbols. For example:

$$\supset \epsilon \epsilon \Im \Im \supset \epsilon \epsilon \Im \Im \supset \epsilon \epsilon \Im \Im \ldots$$

This pattern follows the rule: "*A group of symbols* $\supset$ ϵ ϵ $\Im$ $\Im$ *repeats over and over*".

A sequence is an ordered collection of objects, with possible repetitions. Like any set, it contains members (also called elements, or terms). For example:

1. **1, 1, 2, 3, 5, 8, 13, ...** is the Fibonacci sequence. The first two terms are defined to be 1 and 1, and starting from the third term, each term is equal to the sum of two preceding terms.
2. **2, 5, 8, 11, 14, ...** is a sequence follows the rule N = 3n – 1, where N is the term and n is the position of the term in the sequence. Therefore, N = 3n – 1 is the formula to find the nth term of the sequence.

An average (also known as a mean) is the sum of all the numbers in the set divided by how many of them are in the set.

A median is the middle number in an ordered set, if the set has an odd number of elements. If there is an even number of elements, a median is the average of the two middle numbers of the set.

Sample Problems

1. **15, 16, 23, 40, 51** is a set of 5 numbers. What is the average of the set?

Solution

The sum of the numbers is (15 + 16 + 23 + 40 + 51) = 145. There are five numbers in the set, so the average is 145 ÷ 5 = **29**.

2. If the average of 17 consecutive **odd** numbers is 29, what is the smallest number in the set?

Solution

When you are given a set of *consecutive numbers*, the average is the number that is in the middle of the set (if there is an odd number of terms) or the average of two middle terms (if there is an even number of terms). Therefore, 29 is the middle number of the set.

Since there are 17 numbers total, there must be 8 odd numbers before 29 and 8 odd numbers after 29. Since the difference between each two subsequent numbers in the set is 2, the smallest number in the set is 8 steps of size 2 below the middle number. We can write that as:

$$29 - 2 \cdot 8 = 13$$

Therefore, the smallest number of the set is 13.

Alternatively, you can simply write out the full set of numbers:

13, 15, 17, 19, 21, 23, 25, 27, **29**, 31, 33, 35, 37, 39, 41, 43, 45

Practice Problems

1. Tim received the average score of 82 for his first 4 tests in Science. Which score does he need to get for the 5th final test if he wants to have the average of 85?

   A. 98
   B. 97
   C. 92
   D. 88

2. The average of 10 integers is equal to −11. What is the sum of these integers?

   E. −11
   F. −55
   G. −110
   H. 110

3. Find the 4th term of the sequence: −2, 1, 7, _, 43, …

   A. 14
   B. 19
   C. 17
   D. 15

4. The average of the first 3 numbers of the set is 17 and the average of the next 5 numbers of the same set is 25. What is the average of the set of all 8 numbers?

   E. 4
   F. 11
   G. 13
   H. 22

5. The average of two multiples of 7 is 28. Find the larger number if it is 7 times greater than the smaller.

   A. 28
   B. 35
   C. 42
   D. 49

6. The sum of the first 9 smallest positive integers is not divisible by

   E. 3
   F. 9
   G. 6
   H. 15

7. The product of the first 10 consecutive prime numbers is not divisible by

   A. 25
   B. 22
   C. 6
   D. 2

8. Each term of the sequence is the nonnegative difference of two preceding terms. Find the missing term: 15, 7, 8, 1, 7, 6, _, 5, 4, …

   E. 0
   F. 1
   G. 2
   H. 7

9. In the repeating decimal 0.472819472819472819..., what is the 32nd digit after the decimal point?
   A. 1
   B. 2
   C. 4
   D. 7

10. If the average of 6 distinct positive integers is 11, what is the largest possible integer could be one of these integers?

   E. 61
   F. 51
   G. 41
   H. 31

11. What is the 6th term of this pattern: 0.1, 0.02, 0.12, 0.14, 0.26, _, …

   A. 0.4
   B. 0.3
   C. 0.7
   D. 0.9

12. Which expression can be used to find the value of the nth term of the pattern described by the table below?

Term	1	2	3	4	5	6	…	n
Value	8	6	4	2	0	-2	…	?

   E. $8n$
   F. $2n + 2$
   G. $10 - 2n$
   H. $2n - 1$

13. What is the average of 4 smallest positive multiples of 4?

    A. 10
    B. 8
    C. 4
    D. 2

14. What is the 10th term of the following pattern: $2a + 3, 4a + 6, 6a + 9, \ldots$

    E. $2a - 10$
    F. $12a + 15$
    G. $16a + 18$
    H. $20a + 30$

15. Which number cannot be equal to the average of any two prime numbers?

    A. 15
    B. 13.5
    C. 13
    D. 6.5

16. What is the 100th term of this pattern:
    A123B123C123A123B123C123A123...

    E. A
    F. B
    G. 2
    H. 3

17. What is the difference between the mean and the median of any 17 consecutive integers?

    A. 0
    B. 0.5
    C. 1
    D. 2

18. Which number cannot be the difference between two consecutive perfect squares?

    E. 17
    F. 29
    G. 41
    H. 44

19. If you rearrange the set of integers $\{-4, 27, -34, -23, 3, 1, 0\}$ in order from smallest to largest, which number will be in the middle?

    A. 1
    B. −34
    C. 3
    D. 0

20. What is the range of 23 consecutive multiples of 3?

    E. 27
    F. 60
    G. 66
    H. 69

21. If A & B = A² – B  (– 2) & (– 1).

  A. 5
  B. –5
  C. –4
  D. 1

22. What is the 20ᵗʰ decimal digit of the repeating fraction 3/7?

  E. 4
  F. 2
  G. 5
  H. 1

23. Find the missing term of the pattern:
A, D, G, J, M, _, S, V, Y

  A. N
  B. Q
  C. P
  D. R

24. Which rule for the nth term describes the pattern: 97, 94, 91, 88, … ?

  E. $3n$
  F. $3n$ - 2
  G. $90n + 7$
  H. $100 - 3n$

25. If a + b + c + d = 420, what is the average of a, b, c, and d?

  A. 210
  B. 105
  C. 21
  D. Cannot be determined

In this lesson:

Definitions of a ratio and a proportion: comparing quantities with division.

Definition of a percentage: percentage as a kind of ratio.

What you must know

Definitions

A ratio is a way of comparing two numbers or quantities of items by using division. For example, consider the following set of triangles and circles:

In this set, the ratio of the number of triangles to the number of circles is 4 to 6, or 2 to 3 (4/6 = 2/3). One can also say that *for every 2 triangles, there are 3 circles.*

A proportion is a statement about an equivalency between two ratios. In the example above, the statement 2/3 = 4/6 is a statement of proportionality. Proportions may also be expressed with unknown quantities, where you may be asked to find the unknown. For example: x/3 = 6/9.

A percentage is a ratio expressed in terms of fractions of 100. For example, 1% is 1/100, 10% is 10/100, and so on.

Sample Problems

1. A bag contains 3 red marbles, 11 yellow marbles, and 7 green marbles. What is the ratio of the number of green marbles to the number of non-green marbles in the bag?

   A. 2:1   **B.** 7:13   **C.** 1:2   **D.** 7:11   **E.** 7:3

Solution

The total number of non-green marbles is 3 + 11 = 14. Therefore, the ratio of the number of green to the number of non-green marbles is 7:14, or **C. 1:2** when simplified.

2. Which of the following statements of proportion is true?

   A. 2:8 = 1:7   **B.** 51:68 = 1:3   **C.** 51:68 = 3:4   **D.** 5:15=1:4   **E.** 1:3 = 2:4

Solution

Since 51 = 17 · 3 and 68 = 17 · 4, in the ratio 51:68, both sides can be divided by 17 to obtain an equivalent ratio of 3:4. Therefore, the statement of proportion **B. 51:68 = 1:3** is true.

3. The price of a shirt is lowered by 40%. Later, it is lowered again, by 10%. What single price reduction are these two price reductions equivalent to?

   A. 0%   **B.** 50%   **C.** 30%   **D.** 46%   **E.** 54%

Solution

The easiest way to approach this problem is to assign a convenient price to the shirt. The easiest price to work with is $100. A reduction of 40% from a price of $100 is $100 - $100· (40/100) = $100 - $40 = $60. A further reduction of 10% from that price is $60 - $60 · (10/100) = $60 - $6 = $54. Therefore, the difference between the original price of $100 and the final price is $100 - $54 = $46. This represents the total reduction in price, which is $46/$100 = 46/100 = **D. 46%.**

Practice Problems

1. The height of a rectangle is twice its width. What is the ratio of the height of this rectangle to its perimeter?

   A. 2 : 7
   B. 7 : 12
   C. 7 : 2
   D. 1 : 3

2. If $a : b = 3 : 5$, what is the ratio of $10b$ to $6a$?

   E. 25 : 9
   F. 1 : 1
   G. 5 : 3
   H. 3 : 5

3. If $a : b$ is 1 : 2, and $b : c$ is 1 : 5, what is $a : c$?

   A. 1 : 2
   B. 2 : 5
   C. 1 : 5
   D. 1 : 10

4. If $1 : x$ is equal to 7 : 2, then what is $1 : (x + 2)$?

   E. 16 : 7
   F. 7 : 16
   G. 4 : 7
   H. 9 : 2

5. If the perimeter of a square is equal to the perimeter of an equilateral triangle, what is the ratio of the side of that square to the side of that triangle?

   A. 4 : 7
   B. 7 : 3
   C. 4 : 3
   D. 3 : 4

6. 2 mangos cost as much as 1 pear. 2 pears cost as much as 9 apples. How many apples cost as much as 4 mangos?

   E. 4
   F. 6
   G. 8
   H. 9

7. Which ratio is equivalent to 15% of a number?

   A. 4 : 15
   B. 5 : 33
   C. 3 : 25
   D. 1.5 : 10

8. There are 42 students in a class. Which of the following could be the ratio of the number of boys to the number of girls in this class?

   E. 1 : 4

   F. 2 : 13

   G. 10 : 11

   H. None of the above

9. If 12.7% of N is equal to 347, what is 1.27% of N?

   A. 0.347

   B. 3.47

   C. 34.7

   D. 347

10. The ratio of the number of gray mice to the number of white mice in a cage is 3 : 5. When 3 more gray mice are added to the cage, the new ratio between numbers of gray and white mice becomes 3 : 4. How many mice were in the cage before 3 mice were added?

   E. 16

   F. 24

   G. 32

   H. 35

11. Ben received 3% more votes than Sam during the team captain election. If Ben and Sam were the only two candidates, what percent of all votes did Sam receive?

   A. 47%

   B. 47.5%

   C. 49%

   D. 48.5%

12. The price of a coat increased by 20% in December, and then decreased by 20% three months later. If the final price of the coat was $144, what was the original price of the coat before December?

   E. $120

   F. $150

   G. $160

   H. $144

13. Which number is 12% of one-half of 400?

   A. 24

   B. 25

   C. 28

   D. 96

14. In the pattern: 2, 4, 8, 16, 32, ...,
    what is the ratio of the 5th term to
    the 10th term?

    E. 1 : 32

    F. 1 : 16

    G. 1 : 4

    H. None of the above

15. Which of the following ratios is
    equivalent to 24%?

    A. 24 : 50

    B. 6 : 35

    C. 3 : 25

    D. 12 : 50

16. Which number is the opposite
    reciprocal of 0.5?

    E. 0.5

    F. −5

    G. −2

    H. −0.5

17. After one year, a $1,200 deposit in a
    savings account earning a simple
    interest is worth $1,218. Find the
    annual rate of interest for this
    account.

    A. 2.4%

    B. 2%

    C. 1.8%

    D. 1.5%

18. If one of two integers is 5% of the
    other, and their sum is 63, what is
    their product?

    E. 360

    F. 180

    G. 320

    H. 163

19. If you increase the radius of a circle
    by 50%, what percentage will the
    area of this circle increase by?

    A. 124%

    B. 125%

    C. 120%

    D. 100%

20. If the ratio of *m* to *n* is 7 to 13, then *m* is what percent of (*m* + *n*)?

  E. 83.3%

  F. 80%

  G. 54%

  H. 35%

21. What percentage of the numbers of the following set are prime?

  {1, 2, 3, 4, 5, 6, 7, 8}

  A. 75%

  B. 70%

  C. 62%

  D. 50%

22. What percentage of all multiples of 3 smaller than 25 are prime?

  E. 12.5%

  F. 25%

  G. 5%

  H. 0%

23. 10% of 10% of N is what percentage of N?

  A. 0.01%

  B. 0.1%

  C. 1%

  D. 100%

24. The number N was increased by 20%, and then the result was again increased by 20%. By what percent is the final result greater than the original number?

  E. 44%

  F. 40%

  G. 20%

  H. 10%

25. Which number in the following set is 15% of the sum of all numbers in the set: {7, 9, 11, 13, 20}?

  A. 7

  B. 9

  C. 11

  D. 13

SHSAT Lesson 4: Measurements and Scales

In this lesson:

Measurements: units, square units, unit conversion.
Definition of scale and scale factor: scale drawings.

What you must know

Definitions

A scale drawing or model is a resized copy of an object, when the actual object is too large to be drawn or modeled at actual size.

Consequently, **a scale factor** is the ratio of the dimensions of the object in the drawing to the dimensions of the actual object. The scale factor is written as a ratio between the two dimensions. For example, if a drawing of an object has a scale of 1:20, that means that any line segment in the drawing with some length, would have 20 times the length on the actual object. Thus, a line segment 3 inches long in the drawing would be 60 inches in the actual object.

A square unit is the area of the square with a side of one linear unit. For example, if a square has a side length of 1 inch, its area is equal to 1 square inch, or 1 in^2.

Measurements

Review major and well-known units and basic relationships between them. For example, 1 yard = 3 feet, 1 foot = 12 inches, 1 kilometer = 1000 meters, 1 meter = 100 centimeters, 1 centimeter = 10 millimeters.

Recall relationships between linear (use to measure length), square (used to measure area), and cubic (used to measure volume) units.

Sample Problems

1. A model of a tower is made using a scale of 1 in : 5 ft. If the height of the model tower is 5 inches, what is the actual height of the tower?

Solution

If there are 5 feet in the actual tower for every 1 inch in the model tower, then 5 inches in the model can be written as: 5 in · (5 ft / 1 in) = 25 ft. Therefore, the actual height of the tower is **25 ft**.

2. What is the actual area of the living room in square yards, if in a scale drawing, its dimensions are 9 inches by 6 inches, and its actual length is 13.5 yards?

Solution

First, find the scale factor for the drawing, which is 9 to 13.5, or 2 : 3 (divide both side by 4.5). Keep in mind that the units here are different; the lengths in the drawing are in inches, and the actual lengths are in yards, so the scale factor only applies when you scale between inches and yards.

Use the obtained scale factor to get the actual width of the room:

6 inches · (3 yards / 2 inches) = 9 yards.

Therefore, the actual area of the room is 9 yards · 13.5 yards = **121.5 yd^2**.

Practice Problems

1. On the map, 0.1 inches represents 25 miles. If the real distance between two cities is 112.5 miles, what is the distance between their locations on the map?

   A. 0.45 in
   B. 2 in
   C. 0.2 in
   D. 1 in

2. Two cubes have the volumes of 125 in³ and 64 in³ respectively. What is the ratio of the surface area of the smaller cube to the surface area of the larger cube?

   E. 16 : 25
   F. 4 : 5
   G. 5 : 8
   H. None of the above

3. If on the scale ○○○○○○ is in balance with △△△, than △○○ = ?

   A. ○
   B. △
   C. △△
   D. ○△

4. If the ratio of the areas of two similar triangles is 49 to 81, and the longest side of the larger triangle is 18, what is the longest side of the small triangle?

   E. 16
   F. 14
   G. 12
   H. 7

5. In a scale drawing, 1 cm represents 10 m. On the same diagram, how many square centimeters would represent 1 square meter?

   A. 10
   B. 1
   C. 0.1
   D. 0.01

6. If Tim can do A pull-ups in B seconds, how many pull-ups can he do in C minutes?

   E. 60AC / B
   F. B / (60AC)
   G. AC / B
   H. ABC

12 cm   18 cm

7. Two rectangles in the diagram above are similar. If the area of the first rectangle is 36 cm², what is the area of the second rectangle?

   A. 54 cm²
   B. 16 cm²
   C. 81 cm²
   D. 540 cm²

8. The area of a circle is 625 yd². A second circle has a radius equal to one-fifth of the first circle's radius. What is the area of the second circle?

   E. 16 yd²
   F. 25 yd²
   G. 100 yd²
   H. 125 yd²

9. If an object travels at 6 feet per second, how many yards does it travel in an hour?

   A. 180
   B. 360
   C. 1800
   D. 7200

10. On a scale drawing, the length of an image of a field is 3 times its width. What is the area of the real field, if its length is 45 m?

    E. 675 m²
    F. 600 m²
    G. 360 m²
    H. 135 m²

11. An engineer created a drawing of a rectangular region. The dimensions of the drawing are 4 inches by 11 inches. If the area of the real region is 9900 square meters, what is the scale factor of the drawing?

    A. 1 in : 225 m
    B. 1 in : 25 m
    C. 1 in : 15 m
    D. 1 in : 1.5 m

12. The area of a smaller circle is one twenty-fifth of the area of a larger circle. What is the ratio of the radius of the larger circle to the radius of the smaller circle?

    E. 1 : 25
    F. 5 : 1
    G. 1 : 5
    H. None of the above

13. In order to make 7 quarts of green paint, you need 4 quarts of yellow paint and 3 quarts of blue paint. If you have 20 quarts of yellow paint and can buy enough blue paint, what is the largest amount of green paint you can make?

    A. 490 qt
    B. 350 qt
    C. 140 qt
    D. 35 qt

14. A map in the book has a scale of 1 cm : 5 km. The map has been further scaled down so that 2 cm on the original map corresponds to 1 cm on the new map. What is the scale factor of the new map?

    E. 1 cm : 10 km
    F. 0.5 cm : 10 km
    G. 1 cm : 2.5 km
    H. None of the above

15. David is building a rectangular play space for his cat. The dimensions of the play space are 3 ft by 5 ft. If he increases each side by 10%, what percentage will then the area of the play space increase by?

    A. 21%
    B. 10%
    C. 1%
    D. 0.1%

16. If you want to increase the area of a square from 16 in² to 25 in², then by what percent do you need to increase each side of the square?

    E. 25%
    F. 20%
    G. 12%
    H. 3%

17. If 1 m² = 100 dm², then how many m² is 5 dm²?

    A. 0.04 m²
    B. 0.05 m²
    C. 0.1 m²
    D. 5 m²

18. What scale factor could be used for a map, if the real area of 1 mi² needs to be equal to 0.25 in² on the map?

    E. 1 in : 0.25 mi
    F. 1 mi : 0.5 in
    G. 1 in : 2 mi
    H. None of these

19. If 1 Ukrainian hryvnia (UH) is equal to $0.43, then how many dollars can you get for 129 UH?

    A. $300
    B. $150
    C. $55.47
    D. $43

20. The lengths of two corresponding sides of two similar triangles are 12 cm and 4 cm. By what percentage is the area of the large triangle bigger than the area of the small triangle?

    E. 66%

    F. 200%

    G. 300%

    H. 800%

21. When Katie bought gasoline, she paid $25.20 for 9 gallons. What is the price of 1 gallon of gasoline?

    A. $3

    B. $2.80

    C. $2.78

    D. $1.80

22. If the volume of the model of a can is 12 in³, and the volume of the real can is 96 in³, what is the scale factor of the model?

    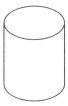

    E. 1 : 12

    F. 2 : 11

    G. 1 : 2

    H. 1 : 0.2

23. Two villages are 24 miles apart. The scale of the map of the region is 0.2 inch to 3 miles. What is the distance between the locations of the two villages on the map?

    A. 72 in

    B. 4.8 in

    C. 1.6 in

    D. 0.8 in

24. The line segment is parallel to the base of the triangle and connected the midpoints of two other sides. What is the ratio of the area of the original triangle to the area of the small one?

    E. 1 : 4

    F. 2 : 3

    G. 4 : 1

    H. 1 : 2

25. In a scale drawing, 0.1 in represents 2 miles. On the same diagram, how many square inchers would represent 1 square mile?

    A. 20

    B. 2

    C. 0.2

    D. 0.0025

SHSAT Lessons 5: Angles.

In this lesson:

Types of angles: supplementary and complementary angles, congruent angles, adjacent angles, vertical angles.

Angle formation: angles formed with two parallel lines and a transversal.

Angles in polygons: the sum of the angles of a triangle or any polygon, exterior angles.

Triangles: the rules for the sides, special triangles.

What you must know:

Definitions

Supplementary angles are two angles whose sum is equal to 180 degrees.

Complementary angles are two angles whose sum is equal to 90 degrees.

Congruent angles are two angles with the same measurement. **Adjacent angles** share a common vertex and side. **Vertical angles** are formed when two lines intersect.

Angles formed with two parallel lines and a transversal: if any transversal intersects two parallel lines, then any two acute angles formed at intersections are congruent; any two obtuse angles formed at intersections are congruent; and any one obtuse angle and any one acute angle formed at intersections are supplementary.

Interior and exterior angles of a triangle and any polygon: the sum of all interior angles of any triangle is 180°. The measure of any exterior angle of the triangle is equal to the sum of measures of two remote interior angles (interior angles that aren't adjacent to the given exterior angle).

For an n-sided polygon, the sum of all interior angles is $S(n) = 180°(n - 2)$, where n is the number of sides. **The sum of all exterior angles** of any polygon (taking only one for each vertex) is 360°.

The rule for triangle sides: any side of any triangle is more than the difference and less than the sum of two other sides.

Special triangles' properties:

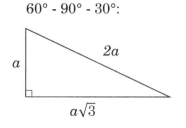

Sample Problems

1. If the sum of two exterior angles of a triangle is 300°, what is the largest possible measure of one of the interior angles of this triangle?

Solution

Since the sum of all exterior angles of any triangle is 360°, we can find the measure of the third exterior angle: 360° − 300° = 60°, and the interior angle which makes the linear pair with 60° is 120° (180° − 60° = 120°). A triangle can have only one obtuse angle, so the largest possible measure of one of the interior angles of this triangle is **120°**.

2. Two right triangles ACD and ADB share side AD. If AC = DC, and AB = 8, find the area of the triangle ACD.

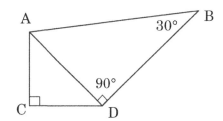

Solution

Both triangles are special: ADB is 30°-90°-60° and ACD is 45°-90°-45°. AD is the leg opposite to 30° angle and AD is equal to one half of AB, thus AD = 4. AC = DC = $2\sqrt{2}$ and the area of the triangle ACD = (1/2) $(2\sqrt{2})(2\sqrt{2})$ = **4**.

3. In the quadrilateral KLMN, if LM = 7, MN = 4, NK = 4, and the perimeter of the KLMN is an integer, what is the largest possible value of the perimeter?

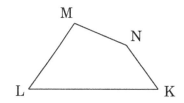

Solution

KL < LM + MN + NK, so KL < 7 + 4 + 4 → KL < 15. The largest possible integer value for KL is 14, and therefore the largest possible integral perimeter is 14 + 15 = **29**.

4. One of the base interior angles of an isosceles trapezoid is 70°. What is the measure of the larger angle between two angle bisectors of the base interior angles of the trapezoid?

Solution

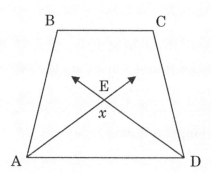

We are given that the measure of the angle BAD and the measure of the angle CDA are 70°. Bisectors AE and DE divide each angle into two equal parts of 35°.
Add all angles of triangle AED to get an equation: $35° + x + 35° = 180°$, and find that $x = 110°$. x is the larger of the two supplementary angles, so the answer is **110°**.

5. Three interior angles of the triangle are consecutive multiples of 3. Find the smallest angle of the triangle.

Solution

Let the smallest interior angle be x, which means that the other two interior angles are $x + 3°$ and $x + 6°$ (consecutive multiples of 3 are 3 units apart). Now write the equation expressing the sum of all three interior angles: $x + (x + 3) + (x + 6) = 180°$. $3x + 9° = 180°$, and $x = $ **57°**.

Practice Problems

1. What is the difference between the sum of all interior angles of any decagon and the sum of all interior angles of any pentagon?

   A. 540°
   B. 720°
   C. 900°
   D. 1080°

2. If one of the angles of a triangle is equal to 110°, what is the average measure of the other two angles?

   E. 35°
   F. 36°
   G. 38°
   H. 55°

3. If one of the exterior angles of a triangle is equal to 142°, what is the sum of the two remote interior angles of this triangle?

   A. 38°
   B. 142°
   C. 168°
   D. 180°

4. The complement of an angle is one-fifth of the measure of the angle itself. What is the measure of the angle?

   E. 15°
   F. 18°
   G. 25°
   H. 75°

5. What is the average of all exterior angles of the decagon?

   A. 28°
   B. 32°
   C. 36°
   D. 288°

6. If two sides of triangle ABC are AB = 12 in and BC = 7 in, which value cannot represent the perimeter of this triangle?

   E. 37 in
   F. 33 in
   G. 26 in
   H. 24 in

7. What is the measure of an acute angle between two diagonals of the regular pentagon that originate from the same vertex?

   A. 24°

   B. 26 °

   C. 28°

   D. 36°

8. Find x in the diagram below.

   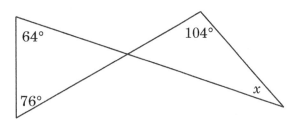

   E. 16°

   F. 28°

   G. 36°

   H. 66°

9. ABCD is a square. M is the midpoint of CD. Find the measure of angle y, if the measure of angle MAD is 32°.

   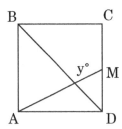

   A. 83°

   B. 87 °

   C. 87°

   D. 103°

10. In the equilateral triangle MNP, MQ is perpendicular to NK and NP is perpendicular to MK. What is the measure of angle n°?

    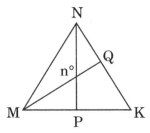

    E. 110°

    F. 120°

    G. 130°

    H. 140°

11. What is the measure of the angle between the hour and minute hands of a clock at 8:20 AM?

    A. 90°

    B. 100°

    C. 110°

    D. 130°

12. What is the difference between the average measure of all angles of a trapezoid and the measure of one angle of a rectangle?

    E. 0°

    F. 6°

    G. 10°

    H. 26°

13. EF is the diameter and CG is the tangent of a circle. If EG is 12 inches, what is the circumference of the circle?

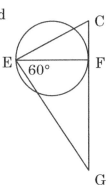

   A. 36π

   B. 12π

   C. 6π

   D. 3π

14. If the angle is 3 times bigger than its supplement, what is the difference between these two angles?

   E. $75°$

   F. $60°$

   G. $90°$

   H. $135°$

15. ABC is a right isosceles triangle and CD is an arc with the center at vertex A. If BC is 8 cm, what is the area of the sector (part of a circle) inside the triangle?

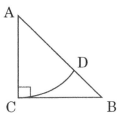

   A. 36π

   B. 8π

   C. 6π

   D. 3π

16. If the sum of two different exterior angles of the triangle is 266°, what is the measure of one of the interior angles of this triangle?

   E. $74°$

   F. $84°$

   G. $86°$

   H. $106°$

17. In the diagram below, find x.

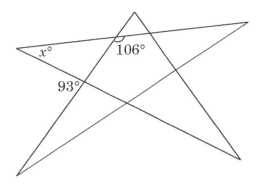

   A. $19°$

   B. $29°$

   C. $41°$

   D. $44°$

18. In the isosceles triangle ABC, AB = BC, and BD = AC = AD. Find the measure of angle ABC.

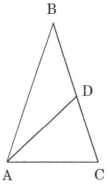

E. 66°

F. 50°

G. 46°

H. 36°

19. Two sides of the triangle are 6 and 11. If each side has the integral measure, what is the largest possible perimeter of the triangle?

A. 23

B. 27

C. 33

D. 37

20. Find the sum of $a° + b°$.

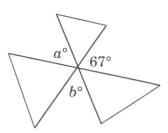

E. 67°

F. 113°

G. 123°

H. 133°

21. In the diagram below, If BD is perpendicular to AC, AD = BD and BC = 2BD, find the measure of an angle ABC.

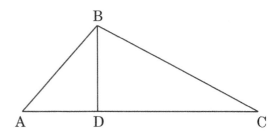

A. 90°

B. 96°

C. 98°

D. 105°

22. Two bisectors of angles A and B of the triangle ABC intersect each other at point P. If the measure of angle C of the triangle is 86°, what is the measure of angle APB?

E. 94°

F. 104°

G. 124°

H. 133°

23. Pentagon ABCDE consists of the square ABDE and an isosceles triangle BCD. If the measure of angle BCD is 112°, what is the measure of angle ADC?

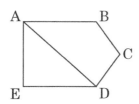

A. 93°

B. 79°

C. 76°

D. 74°

24. All sides of a triangle are integers. If one side is 12, what is the smallest possible difference between the two other sides?

E. 15

F. 7

G. 1

H. 0

25. If the ratio of the three angles of the triangle is 4 : 5 : 9, what kind of the triangle is it?

A. Isosceles

B. Right

C. Acute

D. Obtuse

SHSAT Lessons 6: Problem Solving Strategies.

In this lesson:

Graphic approach: visualizing with pictures, drawing diagrams.

Pattern recognition: repetitions, sequences, regularities.

Substitution: plugging in numbers, replacing variables with numbers.

Solving strategies: working backwards, solving a special case or a simpler problem, checking all possible cases, writing out an equation.

What you must know:

The more problem-solving strategies you know, the better equipped you'll be to answer SHSAT questions quickly and effectively. Often, it can help to use more than one solving strategy on any given problem. In the sample problems, we explore some of the strategies listed above.

Sample Problems

Drawing a Diagram

1. Max used 1/5th of his envelopes on Monday, and 1/4th of the remaining envelopes on Tuesday. How many envelopes did he have in the beginning, if he now has 30 envelops
    left over?

Solution

Represent the total number of envelopes with a bar graph. Since you know that on Monday Max used 1/5th of the envelopes, divide the bar into 5 equal parts and mark one of them as used:

Now note that there are 4 parts left, and recall that Max next used 1/4th of the remaining envelopes. Therefore, you can mark one of the leftover parts as used:

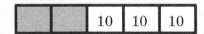

Solution (continued)

Finally, note that the 3 parts left correspond to 30 envelopes. Therefore, each part in the graph above is equal to 10 envelopes. Since there were originally 5 parts, Max originally had 5 x 10 = **50 envelopes**.

Recognizing a pattern in a sequence

2. If the given pattern continues, which fraction will be in the 30th position?

$$\frac{2}{5}, \frac{7}{10}, \frac{12}{15}, \frac{17}{20}, \frac{22}{25}, \cdots$$

Solution

Observe the denominators and note that they are consecutive multiples of 5. Furthermore, note that in each fraction, the numerator is 3 less than the denominator. Therefore, the denominator of the 30th term will be equal to $5 \cdot 30$ = 150 and the numerator will be 150 – 3 = 147. Thus, the 30th fraction in the pattern will be $\frac{147}{150}$.

Number substitution

3. What is the largest possible product of a and b, if $-8 \le a \le -2$ and $-4 \le b \le 1$?

Solution

Among the possible values for a and b, choose the ones with the greatest magnitude (absolute value) – since the product of two negative numbers is positive. $ab = (-8)(-4) = $ **32**.

Observing regularities

4. Find the two missing numbers from the table:

10	15	20	25	30	35	40	45	50	55
1	6	2	7	3	8	?	9	5	?

Solution

Observe the two numbers in each column, and note that each number in the second row is the sum of the digits of the number in the first row. Therefore, the missing numbers are 4 + 0 = **4**, and 5 + 5 = **10**.

Working backwards

5. Sam chose a positive integer less than 20. He multiplied the chosen integer by 6 and then divided it by 2. He then divided the result by 3 and multiplied it by 5. If at the end he got 35, find the integer he started with.

Solution

Suppose Sam chose the number N. Combine the listed operations and write them as an equation: $N \cdot 6 \cdot \frac{1}{2} \cdot \frac{1}{3} \cdot 5 = 5N = 35$, and N = 7.

Or work backwards and perform the listed operations in an opposite order:
$35 \div 5 = 7 \rightarrow 7 \cdot 3 = 21 \rightarrow 21 \cdot 2 = 42 \rightarrow 42 \div 6 = \mathbf{7}$.

Writing out an equation

6. If I had twice the amount of money I have now, I could buy 4 lollipops for 75 cents each and get $1 change. How much money do I have now?

Solution

Write the verbal description in the problem as an equation. Calling the amount of money I have x, "twice the amount of money I have now" is $2x$. "4 lollipops for 75 cents each" is a dollar quantity of 4 · $0.75, and there is also a $1 change, which means that we can write 2x = 4 · $0.75 + $1. Therefore, $2x$ = $4, and x = **$2**.

Practice Problems

1. James solved 1/4th of his homework problems in 15 minutes. In the next 15 minutes, he solved 1/3rd of the remaining problems. If James has 12 more problems left after that, how many problems were there in his homework?

   A. 40
   B. 36
   C. 30
   D. 24

2. Mrs. Wagner spent one-third of her money in one store, and then one-half of the remaining money in another store. How much money did Mrs. Wagner have in the beginning, if she returned home with $17?

   E. $68
   F. $64
   G. $51
   H. $17

3. The perimeter of a rectangle is 6 times as large as the width of the rectangle. How many times is the perimeter of this rectangle larger than its length?

   A. $\frac{1}{3}$
   B. $\frac{1}{2}$
   C. 2
   D. 3

4. If k is an even number, what is the remainder when $(k + 2)^2$ is divided by 4?

   E. 0
   F. 1
   G. 2
   H. 3

5. The number of bacteria in a bacterial culture doubles every 10 minutes. The ratio of the number of bacteria at the end of 1 hour to the number of bacteria at the beginning of that hour is:

   A. 2 : 1
   B. 8 : 1
   C. 64 : 1
   D. 1024 : 1

6. If a set of numbers begins with −11 and every number after that is 10 more the number that comes before it, what is the 100th number in the set?

   E. 959
   F. 969
   G. 979
   H. 989

7. The product of the first 50 prime numbers is not divisible by:

   A. 26
   B. 36
   C. 46
   D. 86

8. Find A, if $A - \frac{1}{2} - \frac{1}{4} = 0$.

   E. 0.625
   F. 0.65
   G. 0.75
   H. −0.75

9. Simplify:
   $(t + 1) - (t - 3) + (t + 5) - (t - 7) + \ldots$
   $\ldots + (t + 17) - (t - 19) =$

   A. $19t - 100$
   B. $t + 190$
   C. $t - 190$
   D. 100

10. If p and q are integers, and $p^2 = 1$, $q^2 = 81$, what is the smallest possible value of $(q - p)$?

   E. −10
   F. −8
   G. 0
   H. −1

11. If the numerator of a fraction is 1 greater than its denominator, but smaller than 20, which of these is the largest possible value of this fraction?

   A. $\frac{3}{2}$
   B. $\frac{4}{3}$
   C. $\frac{11}{10}$
   D. $\frac{21}{20}$

12. For how many different integer values of N is $\frac{6}{N}$ also an integer?

   E. 8
   F. 7
   G. 5
   H. 4

13. Steve entered an elevator on a certain floor. Then the elevator moved up 7 floors, down 8 floors, and up 3 floors. On what floor did Steve initially enter the elevator, if he is now at floor 10?

   A. 9
   B. 8
   C. 6
   D. 4

14. I began with my favorite number, subtracted 7 from it, multiplied the result by 3, and then added 2 to that. My final result is 20. What is my favorite number?

    E. 17
    F. 13
    G. 5
    H. 1

15. Ann had a roll of fabric. She used $\frac{1}{2}$ of the roll, then $\frac{1}{2}$ of the remaining amount, and then $\frac{1}{2}$ of the remaining amount again. She now has 7 yards left over. How many yards of fabric did she have in the beginning?

    A. 64 yards
    B. 60 yards
    C. 56 yards
    D. 40 yards

16. The 3-digit number 103 has a digit-sum of $1 + 0 + 3 = 4$. How many different 3-digit whole numbers, including 103, have a digit sum of 4?

    E. 6
    F. 7
    G. 9
    H. 10

17. Find the largest factor of 1260 that is not divisible by 6.

    A. 630
    B. 315
    C. 210
    D. 63

18. When a certain number is divided by 5, the result is the same as when this number decreased by 12. What is this number?

    E. 20
    F. 15
    G. 5
    H. -15

19. Kathy has $13 more than Jack and $3 less than Vanessa. All together, Kathy, Jack, and Vanessa have $59. How much money does Jack have?

    A. $10
    B. $12
    C. $18
    D. $7

20. Tickets for a play cost $6 for a child, and $15 for an adult. A group of 25 people paid a total of $204 for the play. How many children were in this group?

    E. 20
    F. 18
    G. 12
    H. 19

21. If $\wedge\wedge a\wedge\wedge = |a| - \dfrac{1}{a}$, what is the value of $\wedge\wedge(-2)\wedge\wedge$?

    A. −2
    B. −1
    C. 0
    D. 2.5

22. If $b^{\diamond} = -(5b - 3)$, what is the value of $(-7)^{\diamond}$?

    E. 38
    F. −7
    G. 13
    H. −38

23. If $-m - n = 5$ and $m - n = -3$, what is the value of $m^2 - n^2$?

    A. 2
    B. −2
    C. 15
    D. −15

24. If the length of a rectangle is multiplied by 3, and the width of a rectangle is multiplied by 2, the area of the rectangle will be N times bigger. What is N?

    E. 6
    F. 3
    G. 2
    H. Cannot be determined

25. The price for a coat was reduced 3 times, each time by 20% from the price that preceded it. What is the total percentage of price reduction from the original price of the coat?

    A. 60%
    B. 51.2%
    C. 48.8%
    D. Cannot be determined

SHSAT Lessons 7: Probability and Combinatorics

In this lesson:

Basic Probability: Outcomes. Sample Space.
Combinatorics: Permutations. Combinations. Dirichlet's principle.

What you must know

Definitions

Sample Space is the list of all possible outcomes (or events) that can occur.

Probability is the ratio (or fraction) of favorable outcomes to the total numbers of possible outcomes. Typically, the chance that an event or series of events will occur is expressed on a scale from 0 (impossible) to 1 (certainty) or as an equivalent percentage from 0 to 100%.

Dirichlet's box principle states that if n items are put into m boxes and $n > m$ (which is to say that the number of items is greater than number of boxes), then at least one box will contain more than one item. For example, if you have 5 rabbits and you put them in 4 cages, it's guaranteed that one cage would contain more than one rabbit.

Sample Problems

1. You have four coins: a quarter, a dime, a nickel, and a penny. You are making different fractions with the cent value of one coin in the numerator and the cent value of another coin in the denominator. How many fractions with distinct values can you make?

Solution

Write out an organized list, starting with all fractions with 1 in the numerator (and listing them by the value in the denominator), and so on.

$$\frac{1}{5}, \frac{1}{10}, \frac{1}{25}, \frac{5}{1}, \frac{5}{10}, \frac{5}{25}, \frac{10}{1}, \frac{10}{5}, \frac{10}{25}, \frac{25}{1}, \frac{25}{5}, \frac{25}{10}.$$

There are $3 \times 4 = 12$ outcomes, but we have 2 pairs of fractions with equal values: $\frac{1}{5} = \frac{5}{25}$ and $\frac{25}{5} = \frac{5}{1}$, so each of them only counts once. Therefore, the answer is **10**.

2. If you randomly pick a day in January, what is the greatest possible probability that the chosen day is Sunday?

Solution

There can be 4 or 5 Sundays in January (depends on what day of the week January 1 is). Therefore, the probability of randomly picking a Sunday is either $\frac{5}{31}$ or $\frac{4}{31}$. Since $\frac{5}{31} > \frac{4}{31}$, the answer is $\frac{5}{31}$.

3. A room contains 10 cats and 15 small toys. Each cat is playing with at least one toy, but with no more than 2 toys. If all toys are being played with, how many cats are playing with 2 toys?

Solution

If each cat is given 1 toys, there are 5 toys left. Since all toys are in play, these five toys are being played with. But since each cat cannot have more than 2 toys, exactly **5 cats** have 2 toys.

4. If $|x| = 2$, and $|y| = 3$, and the signs of x and y are randomly selected, what is the probability that $|x + y| = 1$?

Solution

Since x could be 2 or –2, and y could be 3 or –3, the sum of x and y could be 5, –5, 1, or –1, which means that $|x + y|$ could be 5 or 1.

Therefore, the probability of getting 1 is 1 out of 2, or $\frac{1}{2}$.

5. If the probability of picking a white marble from a bag is $\frac{3}{4}$, and there are 12 white marbles in the bag, how many marbles in the bag are not white?

Solution

There are 12 white marbles in the bag and they constitute $\frac{3}{4}$ of all marbles. Therefore, the number of non-white marbles is $1 - \frac{3}{4} = \frac{1}{4}$ of the total. Since we know that $\frac{3}{4}$ of the total is 12, $\frac{1}{4}$ of the total is 3 times less, or $12 \div 3 = \mathbf{4}$.

Practice Problems

1. There are 4 red and 5 yellow marbles in the bag. If you pick 2 marbles without looking, what is the probability that both marbles you picked are red?

   A. $\frac{1}{3}$

   B. $\frac{1}{4}$

   C. $\frac{1}{6}$

   D. $\frac{1}{9}$

2. The locker's combination code consists of one letter and 3 digits. How many possible different codes exist, if the letter can be A or C and must come first, and the digits can be repeated?

   E. 600

   F. 1200

   G. 1500

   H. 2000

3. 2 boys and 2 girls are sitting around a square table. Each seat is numbered 1, 2, 3, and 4. How many different arrangements of the 4 children are possible?

   A. 4

   B. 16

   C. 24

   D. 32

4. There are 25 students in a class. What is the smallest number of children that are guaranteed to have their birthdays in the same month?

   E. 0

   F. 1

   G. 2

   H. 3

5. There are 3 small cubes in the bag: red, blue and green. You are picking cubes from the bag one by one. What is the chance that you'll pick the red cube last?

   A. $\frac{1}{3}$

   B. $\frac{1}{5}$

   C. $\frac{1}{9}$

   D. $\frac{2}{9}$

6. The target consists of three concentric circles with the radii 1, 2, and 3 units respectively. If a dart hits the target randomly, what is the probability of hitting the innermost circle on the first shot?

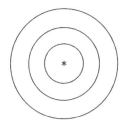

   E. $\frac{1}{3}$

   F. $\frac{2}{3}$

   G. $\frac{1}{5}$

   H. $\frac{1}{9}$

7. If you write down all positive integers from 1 to 50, what is the total number of times that 3 and 7 will appear on paper?

   A. 20
   B. 18
   C. 8
   D. 7

8. Find the largest factor of 1568 that is not divisible by 7.

   E. 254
   F. 392
   G. 32
   H. 98

9. Two boys and three girls want to sit in a row of 5 chairs. How many possible arrangements exist, if a boy always sits in the first and the last chair?

   A. 24
   B. 12
   C. 6
   D. 2

10. How many three-digit positive numbers have only odd digits?

   E. 125
   F. 60
   G. 28
   H. 24

11. What is the unit (ones) digit of the number 3^{13} ?

   A. 1
   B. 3
   C. 9
   D. 8

12. Which integer of the ones below has the largest number of prime factors?

   E. 143
   F. 140
   G. 130
   H. 128

13. How many more prime numbers are between 10 and 30 than between 10 and 20?

   A. 1
   B. 2
   C. 3
   D. 4

14. There are 20 balls, numbered from 1 to 20, in the bag. If you pick one ball from the bag, what is the probability of picking a prime-numbered ball?

   E. $\frac{1}{3}$

   F. $\frac{2}{3}$

   G. $\frac{2}{5}$

   H. $\frac{9}{20}$

15. What is the probability of picking 2 red marbles from the jar that contains 2 blue and 2 red marbles?

   A. $\frac{1}{4}$

   B. $\frac{3}{4}$

   C. $\frac{1}{6}$

   D. $\frac{1}{2}$

16. There are 14 people in the room. What is the probability that at least 2 people have their birthday in the same month?

   E. $\frac{1}{12}$

   F. $\frac{1}{7}$

   G. 1

   H. 0

17. Seven birds are placed into 3 cages. What is the smallest possible number of birds in the cage with the largest number of birds?

   A. 1
   B. 2
   C. 3
   D. 4

18. Repeating fraction $\frac{1}{7}$ was rounded to a random length in its decimal expansion. What is the probability that the last digit in the rounded value is 3?

   E. $\frac{1}{8}$

   F. $\frac{1}{6}$

   G. 1

   H. 0

19. Balls with letters that form the word MATHEMATICS are placed in a bowl. What is the probability of first picking a ball with a letter other than "C" and then picking one with a "C"?

   A. $\frac{3}{4}$

   B. $\frac{1}{12}$

   C. $\frac{1}{10}$

   D. $\frac{1}{11}$

20. In a group of students, 16 got an A in Math, 14 got an A in Science, and 5 got both an A in Math and an A in Science. If a student is selected at random, find the probability, expressed as a percentage, that the student has an A in Math and an A in Science.

   E. 20%

   F. 16%

   G. 14%

   H. 12%

21. If you randomly select a two-digit integer, what is the probability that it is not a multiple of 5?

   A. $\frac{64}{81}$

   B. $\frac{4}{5}$

   C. $\frac{11}{18}$

   D. $\frac{11}{81}$

22. If the letters in the word LATE are randomly rearranged, what is the probability that the resulting word will be TALE?

   E. $\frac{1}{7}$

   F. $\frac{1}{12}$

   G. $\frac{1}{24}$

   H. 0

23. The area of a circle inside a square is equal to $\frac{1}{3}$ of the area of the square. What is the probability that the point randomly selected inside the square will be outside of the circle?

A. $\frac{1}{3}$

B. $\frac{2}{3}$

C. $\frac{1}{8}$

D. $\frac{1}{2}$

24. Mr. Jones has 6 coworkers: 2 men and 4 women. How many different groups of 2 people could be selected for a project if a group must have 1 man and 1 woman?

E. 8

F. 32

G. 24

H. 12

25. You are given two sets, X = {2, 5, 7, 9} and Y = {1, 3, 4, 8}. A number is randomly selected from each set. What is the probability that the sum of the two selected numbers is 10?

A. $\frac{1}{16}$

B. $\frac{2}{3}$

C. $\frac{3}{16}$

D. $\frac{1}{3}$

SHSAT Lesson 8: Coordinate Plane

In this lesson:

Cartesian coordinates: Points, lines, and shapes in a coordinate system.

What you must know

Definitions

The coordinate plane consists of two perpendicular lines: the horizontal **x-axis** (*abscissa*) and vertical **y-axis** (*ordinate*). Point 0 (0, 0) **is the origin**, which can be thought of as a starting point. If you want to place point P (a, b) on the coordinate plane, you would start at the origin and make a steps to the right (if $a > 0$) or to the left (if $a < 0$) and b steps up (if $b > 0$) or down (if $b < 0$).

The plane has **4 quadrants** I, II, III, and IV:

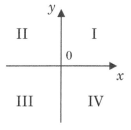

If point P (a, b) is in the first (I) quadrant, a and b are both positive.
If point P (a, b) is in the second (II) quadrant, a is negative, and b is positive.
If point P (a, b) is in the third (III) quadrant, a and b are both negative.
If point P (a, b) is in the fourth (IV) quadrant, a is positive and b is negative.
Any point P (a, b) is a units from the y-axis and b units from the x-axis.

For all problems with coordinates, drawing a graph is very helpful.

Sample Problems

1. Point P (a, b) lies in the second quadrant. Which inequality **must** be true?

   A. $a > b$ **B.** $a = b$ **C.** $a - b < 0$ **D.** $a + b > 0$

Solution

In the second quadrant, the x-coordinate is negative, and y-coordinate is positive. That means a is negative and b is positive. Therefore, (A) and (B) are always false, and while (D) can be true, it may not be (depending on the exact values of a and b). However, $a - b < 0$ is **always** true. Therefore the right answer is (**C**).

2. Which of the following points is the closest to P $(-1, 2)$?

   E. $(-2, 2)$ **F.** $(-1, 1)$ **G.** $(-1, 0)$ **H.** $(-0.5, 2)$

Solution

Note that three of the given points differ by 1 in just one coordinate from P, which means they are 1 unit from P. $(-0.5, 2)$, however, differs from P by just 0.5 in one of the coordinates, which means it's 0.5 units from P. The correct answer is (**H**).

3. Find the area of the triangle KLN, if K $(0, 2)$, L $(-2, 1)$ and N $(0, 7)$.

Solution

It helps to draw the graph and picture the triangle in the coordinate grid. It's convenient to consider the segment MN as a base. The distance from point L to the base MN is the height of triangle KLN. This distance is equal to 2 units, because point L is 2 units from the y-axis, and both points K and N are on the y-axis. KN is the actual base of the triangle, and its length is just the difference in the KN is the actual base of the triangle, and its length is just the difference in the y-coordinates of K and N, which is $(7 - 2)$. Now, using the base $\times$ height / 2 calculation, we determine that the area of the triangle KLN is equal to $(7 - 2) \times 2 / 2 = $ **5 square units**.

4. What is the distance from point P (–5, 7) to point Q, which is the result of the reflection of point P over *y*-axis?

Solution

Point P is 5 units from *y*-axis; therefore, point Q is also 5 units from y-axis. Therefore, PQ = 5 units + 5 units = **10 units.**

Practice Problems

1. Point W (x, y) lies in the fourth quadrant. Which inequality must be true?

   A. $y > x$
   B. $x - y < 0$
   C. $x + y > 0$
   D. $xy < 0$

2. What is the distance from point A $(-8, -2)$ to point B, which is the result of the reflection of point A over x-axis?

   E. 4
   F. 6
   G. 12
   H. 16

3. Find the area of triangle CDE, if C $(5, 0)$, D $(-2, 0)$, and E $(3, 4)$.

   A. 7
   B. 11
   C. 13
   D. 14

4. Point E is the midpoint of the line segment CD, with C $(-2, 0)$ and D $(14, 0)$. Find the coordinates of point E.

   E. $(0, -2)$
   F. $(0, 6)$
   G. $(6, 0)$
   H. $(0, 7)$

5. Which of the following may change when taking an absolute value of a number?

   A. Base
   B. Sign
   C. Precision
   D. Magnitude

6. How many non-overlapping squares with a side of 1 unit and a vertex at the origin could be drawn on the coordinate plane?

   E. None
   F. 2
   G. 4
   H. Infinitely many

7. If you start at the origin and move 4
    units to the right, 4 units up and 4
    units to the left, how far from the
    origin will be your endpoint?

    A. 0 units
    B. 1 unit
    C. 3 units
    D. 4 units

8. What is the point of intersection of
    the vertical line $x = -3$ and
    horizontal line $y = 2$?

    E. (3, −2)
    F. (−3, 2)
    G. (2, −3)
    H. (−2, −3)

9. Find the area of the triangle ABC.

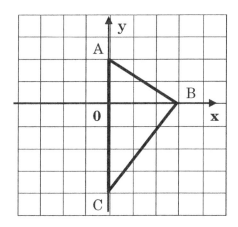

    A. 9 sq. units.
    B. 12 sq. units.
    C. 16 sq. units.
    D. 18 sq. units.

10. Which of the following points is
    closest to the origin?

    E. (0, 3)
    F. (−3, 0)
    G. (2, 2)
    H. (2, 3)

11. What is the area of a square with
    two opposite vertices at M (0, 2) and
    K (0, −2)?

    A. 2 sq. un.
    B. 4 sq. un.
    C. 6 sq. un.
    D. 8 sq. un.

12. Point P (c, d) lies in the third
    quadrant. Which inequality must be
    true?

    E. $c > d$
    F. $c - d < 0$
    G. $cd > 0$
    H. $c + d > 0$

13. What is the distance from the
    midpoint of AB to the midpoint of
    BC, if A (−3, 0), B (−1, 0) and C (7, 0)?

    A. 10
    B. 8
    C. 6
    D. 5

14. Which of the listed figures is closest to the origin?

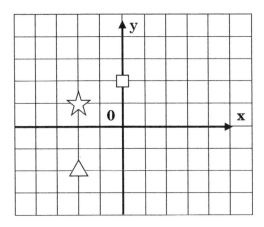

   E. None
   F. Star
   G. Triangle
   H. Square

15. Which two of the listed figures are the same distance from the origin?

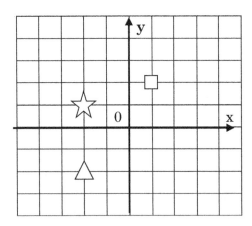

   A. Star and triangle
   B. Star and square
   C. Square and triangle
   D. Cannot be determined

16. What point is exactly 5 units from point A (–1, –2)?

   E. (0, –3)
   F. (–3, 0)
   G. (2, 2)
   H. (–1, –3)

17. The y-axis is the tangent of a circle with center at C (–2, 4). What is the area of the circle?

   A. 16π
   B. 4π
   C. 8π
   D. 3π

18. What is the diameter of a circle with a center at (4, –2), if one of the points on its circumference is (4, 0)?

   E. 4
   F. 5
   G. 6
   H. 7

19. Diagonals of a rhombus are on the x-axis and y-axis respectively. The top vertex is at (0, 8). If each side of the rhombus is 10, what is the area of the rhombus?

   A. 108
   B. 96
   C. 48
   D. 24

20. Which of the points below is closest to the x-axis?

    E. (0, –1)
    F. (–1, 2)
    G. (–1, –2)
    H. (0, 6)

21. Find the perimeter of the triangle KLM.

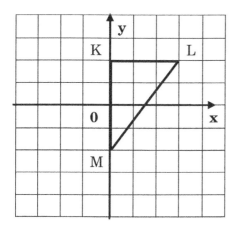

    A. 15
    B. 13
    C. 12
    D. 10

22. How far from the origin is the point D (–6, –8)?

    E. 12
    F. 10
    G. 8
    H. 7

23. Which line is not parallel to the line $y = x$?

    A. $y - x = 2$
    B. $y = x - 7$
    C. $y + x = 4$
    D. $3 - y = -x$

24. The isosceles triangle CDE is on the coordinate plane. What is the area of the triangle?

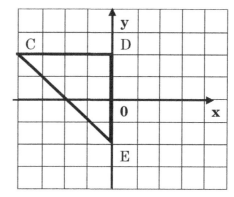

    E. 12
    F. 10
    G. 8
    H. 4

25. If the product of x and y coordinates of a point is negative, this point must be in the:

    A. II quadrant
    B. II or III quadrant
    C. II or IV quadrant
    D. I or IV quadrant

Answers

Lesson 1		Lesson 2		Lesson 3		Lesson 4		Lesson 5		Lesson 6		Lesson 7		Lesson 8	
1.	A	1.	B	1.	D	1.	A	1.	C	1.	D	1.	C	1.	D
2.	H	2.	G	2.	E	2.	E	2.	E	2.	G	2.	H	2.	E
3.	C	3.	B	3.	D	3.	C	3.	B	3.	D	3.	C	3.	D
4.	F	4.	H	4.	F	4.	F	4.	H	4.	E	4.	H	4.	G
5.	B	5.	D	5.	D	5.	D	5.	C	5.	C	5.	A	5.	B
6.	H	6.	G	6.	H	6.	E	6.	H	6.	G	6.	H	6.	H
7.	B	7.	A	7.	D	7.	C	7.	D	7.	B	7.	A	7.	D
8.	E	8.	F	8.	G	8.	F	8.	G	8.	G	8.	G	8.	F
9.	C	9.	D	9.	C	9.	D	9.	D	9.	D	9.	B	9.	A
10.	G	10.	F	10.	G	10.	E	10.	F	10.	E	10.	E	10.	G
11.	C	11.	A	11.	D	11.	C	11.	D	11.	A	11.	B	11.	D
12.	E	12.	G	12.	F	12.	F	12.	E	12.	E	12.	H	12.	G
13.	D	13.	A	13.	A	13.	D	13.	C	13.	B	13.	B	13.	D
14.	H	14.	H	14.	E	14.	E	14.	G	14.	F	14.	G	14.	H
15.	C	15.	B	15.	D	15.	A	15.	B	15.	C	15.	C	15.	B
16.	E	16.	H	16.	G	16.	E	16.	G	16.	H	16.	G	16.	G
17.	C	17.	A	17.	D	17.	B	17.	A	17.	B	17.	C	17.	B
18.	E	18.	H	18.	F	18.	G	18.	H	18.	F	18.	F	18.	E
19.	D	19.	D	19.	B	19.	C	19.	C	19.	A	19.	D	19.	B
20.	E	20.	G	20.	H	20.	H	20.	F	20.	H	20.	E	20.	E
21.	B	21.	A	21.	D	21.	B	21.	D	21.	D	21.	B	21.	C
22.	H	22.	F	22.	E	22.	G	22.	H	22.	E	22.	G	22.	F
23.	D	23.	C	23.	C	23.	C	23.	B	23.	C	23.	B	23.	C
24.	G	24.	H	24.	E	24.	G	24.	H	24.	E	24.	H	24.	G
25.	C	25.	B	25.	B	25.	D	25.	B	25.	C	25.	C	25.	C

Solutions to Practice Questions

Lesson 1

1. A. 135

Since n must be divisible by 9, the sum of all digits in the answer must be divisible by 9. $1 + 3 + 5 = 9$, and therefore the number 135 is divisible by 9.

2. H. 5

$48 = 2 \cdot 2 \cdot 2 \cdot 2 \cdot 3$, which means the two distinct prime factors are 2 and 3 and their sum is $2 + 3 = 5$.

3. C. 560

Out of three consecutive integers, at least one is divisible by 2 and one is divisible by 3. That means that the number we are looking should not be divisible by 2 or by 3.

All answers are divisible by 2, but 560 ($5 + 6 + 0 = 11$) is not divisible by 3 and therefore cannot be the product of three consecutive numbers.

4. F. 53

All answers are within the given interval, but only 53 is the prime.

5. B. 1, 2, 3, 5, 7, 9

We need to remove 4, 6, and 8 from the set, because they are neither prime nor odd. 1, 3, 5, 7, and 9 are odd (3, 5, and 7 are also prime) and 2 is a prime number.

6. H. b − 2

Since $b + 4$ is odd, b must be odd. All choices add or subtract an odd number from an odd number, which produces an even number, except choice H, where an even number is subtracted from an odd number, thus producing another odd number.

7. B. 2y + 3

$2y + 1$ is an odd number for any integer y. Therefore, the next (smallest) odd number will be 2 more than $2y + 1$ or $2y + 3$.

8. E. 16

16 is the only number among possible choices which does not have odd prime factors. (recall that 1 is not prime).

9. C. $2^3 \cdot 3^2$

Use successive splitting into smaller factors to arrive at the answer:

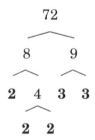

10. G. 36th

The question can be rephrased as: What is the lease common multiple of 9 and 12? The smallest number divisible both by 9 and 12 is 36.

11. C. Distributive

The standard form of the distributive property is $a(b \pm c) = ab \pm ac$.
$4(12 − 7) = 4 \cdot 12 − 4 \cdot 7$ or $4(12 − 7) = 48 − 28$.

12. E. 4

The smallest positive even numbers are 2, 4, and 6. Their average is 4.

13. D. 1

Based on the rules of order of operations we should start with $-9 + 2 = -7$, then $56 \div (-7) = -8$, $(-8) \cdot 3 = -24$. Since $3 \div (-1) = -3$, we will have $-24 - 10 - 3 + 38 = 1$.

14. H. 9

There are 18 integers which are divisible by 11 (because $200 \div 11 = 18r2$) and 9 which are divisible by 3 and by 7 (or by 21: $200 \div (3 \cdot 7) = 200 \div 21 = 9r11$). The difference is $18 - 9 = 9$.

15. C. 43

Since my car is 29th, there are 28 cars in front of my car and $28 \div 2 = 14$ cars are behind. The total is $28 + 14 + 1$ (my own car) $= 43$ cars.

16. E. Must be an even number.

If you divide the number by 2 and the remainder is 0, it means that the number is divisible by 2 or **even**. X therefore must be an even number.

17. C. 1 : 7

Multiply $\frac{a}{b}$ by $\frac{b}{c}$: $\frac{a}{b} \cdot \frac{b}{c} = \frac{a}{c} = \frac{3}{7} \cdot \frac{1}{3} = \frac{1}{7}$.

18. E. 33

Recall that $m^2 - n^2 = (m + n)(m - n)$. Since we know the value of both $m + n$ and $m - n$, we can write $11 \cdot 3 = 33$.

19. D. 36

Factor 120 and all the choices to compare them:
$120 = 2 \cdot 2 \cdot 2 \cdot 3 \cdot 5$
$8 = 2 \cdot 2 \cdot 2$
$15 = 3 \cdot 5$
$30 = 2 \cdot 3 \cdot 5$
$36 = 2 \cdot 2 \cdot 3 \cdot 3$
Note that all of the choices' factors comprise some subset of the factors of 120, except 36, which has an extra factor of 3.

20. E. 41/40

For a fraction to be convertible into a terminating decimal, its denominator (in reduced form) should only have factors of 2 or 5 (because then, both the numerator and denominator can be multiplied by a corresponding number of 2s and 5s to get a power of 10 in the denominator, which results in a decimal fraction). Among the provided answers, only 41/40 has a denominator whose factors are 2, 2, 2, and 5. $41/40 = 1.025$

21. B. 78

$42 = 2 \cdot 3 \cdot 7$, $12 = 2 \cdot 2 \cdot 3$. Therefore, GCF(12, 42) $= 2 \cdot 3 = 6$ and LCM(12, 42) $= 42 \cdot 2 = 84$. The difference is $84 - 6 = 78$.

22. H. 6

If P is a product of two odd numbers, it can never be even. Among the choices, there is only one even number – therefore that's the right answer.

23. D. 73.5

The smallest multiple of 7 in the given interval is 28 and the largest is 119. The multiples of 7 are a sequence, spaced apart by 7. The best way to find the average of all numbers in the sequence is to find the average of 28 and 119 (this works for any sequence of numbers spaced apart by the same interval), which is $(28 + 119) \div 2 = 73.5$.

24. G. 988

The largest 3-digit integer is 999, and we want to find the integer closest to it that is divisible by 13. $999 \div 13 = 76r11$, so the largest integer divisible by 13 is 11 less than 999, which is $999 - 11 = 988$.

25. C. 6

Let's call our integer N. Then, we can write $3N - 5 = 26 \div 2$ or $3N - 5 = 13$. Solve the equation to get $N = 6$.

Lesson 2

1. B. 97

The total number of points Tim received for his first 4 tests is equal to $82 \cdot 4 = 328$. In order to get an 85 average, his total across 5 tests needs to be $85 \cdot 5 = 425$. That means that on the last test, he needs to get $425 - 328 = 97$.

2. G. –110

Average of N numbers is the result of the division of the sum of N numbers by N. Therefore, if we want to find the sum, we need to apply the opposite operation and multiply the average –11 by 10 to get –110.

3. B. 19

The pattern is in increasing each consecutive term by 3, 6, 12, 24,… and so on (doubling the previous addend):

$-2 + 3 = 1$

$1 + 6 = 7$

$7 + 12 = 19$

$19 + 24 = 43$

Therefore, the missing number in the pattern is 19.

4. H. 22

The sum of the first 3 numbers is $17 \cdot 3 = 51$, and the sum of the next 5 is $25 \cdot 5 = 125$. Therefore, the sum of all 8 numbers is $51 + 125 = 176$.

In order to find the average of all 8 numbers we divide 176 by 8:

$176 \div 8 = 22$

5. D. 49

Let the smaller number be x and the larger be $7x$. We know that their average is $(x + 7x) \div 2 = 28$. Solving the equation, we get $8x \div 2 = 28$, $4x = 28$, or $x = 7$.

7 is the smaller number and the larger number is $7 \cdot 7 = 49$.

6. G. 6

The sum $1 + 2 + 3 + 4 + 5 + 6 + 7 + 8 + 9 = (1 + 9) \cdot 4 + 5 = 45$. This sum is not divisible by 6, because 45 is not even.

7. A. 25

The product in question has only one factor of 5, but $25 = 5 \cdot 5$, so 25 cannot be its factor.

8. F. 1

The difference of 2 preceding terms is $7 - 6 = 1$.

9. D. 7

The repeating part of the decimal is 472819 and consists of 6 digits. $32 \div 6 = 5r2$.

The remainder of 2 means that the second digit in the repeating part will be the 32nd digit. The second digit of the repeating part is 7.

10. F. 51

The sum of the six integers is $6 \cdot 11 = 66$. Since all integers must be different, we will should 1, 2, 3, 4, and 5 as the 5 smallest possible integers to maximize the 6th integer. $1 + 2 + 3 + 4 + 5 = 15$, and the 6th and largest possible integer is $66 - 15 = 51$.

11. A. 0.4

Each number in the pattern is the sum of two previous terms. Therefore, the missing term is equal to 0.14 + 0.26 = 0.4.

12. G. 10 − 2n

An easy way is to substitute an easy value for n from the table into each expression and test them. We know that for $n = 5$, the result must be equal to 0. The only choice that satisfies that is 10 − 2n.

13. A. 10

4, 8, 12, and 16 are the 4 smallest positive multiples of 4. The average of these numbers is 10. The quick way to calculate is to only average the endpoints of the sequential number set (4 + 16) ÷ 2 = 10.

14. H. 20a + 30

Each term of the pattern consists of two addends – the first terms in each are consecutive multiples of 2a and the second terms in each are consecutive multiples of 3. Therefore, the 10th term of the pattern is

$$10 \cdot (2a) + 10 \cdot 3 = 20a + 30.$$

15. B. 13.5

If a number X is an average of two numbers, then the sum of these two numbers is 2X. Therefore, the possible sums of two prime numbers derived from the answer choices are 30, 27, 26, and 13. We can see that 30 = 13 + 17 or 11 + 19, and 26 = 23 + 3 or 19 + 7. Notice that an odd sum of two prime numbers

must have 2 as one of the addends (because other than 2, prime numbers are odd, and the sum of two prime numbers that are not 2 will always be even). 13 = 2 + 11, so 13 can be a sum of two prime numbers. But 27 = 2 + 25, and 25 is not a prime number. The sum of 27 corresponds to the average of 13.5.

16. H. 3

Each group has 4 terms, the first is the letter and after that just 123.
Since 100 is divisible by 4, 100th digit will be the same as the last term of each pattern, which is 3.

17. A. 0

For any set of consecutive integers, the mean is equal to the median and the difference between two equal numbers is 0.

18. H. 44

The difference between two consecutive perfect squares must be odd, because one of them is odd and the other is even or vice versa. 4 − 1 = 3; 9 − 4 = 5; 16 − 9 = 7 and so on.
So the difference cannot be even, and the answer is therefore 44.

19. D. 0

Arrange all number in order: −34, −23, −4, 0, 1, 3, 27. The middle number is 0.

20. G. 66

If the first number is T, the 23rd will be T + 22 · 3 or T + 66, because the set has 23 consecutive numbers. The range is the difference between the largest number, T + 66, and the smallest number, T, which is 66.

21. A. 5

Simply substitute the values into the equation, to get:

$(-2)^2 - (-1)^3 = 4 - (-1) = 4 + 1 = 5$.

22. F. 2

$3 \div 7 = 0.428571428571428571\ldots$ The pattern has 6 digits. $20 \div 6 = 3r2$. The remainder of 2 means that the second digit of the pattern group is the 20th decimal digit of the decimal expansion, so the answer is 2.

23. C. P

The pattern is to take every 4th letter of the alphabet, starting with the first one. You can write it out:

<u>A</u> B C <u>D</u> E F <u>G</u> H I <u>J</u> K L <u>M</u> N O <u>P</u> Q R <u>S</u> T U <u>V</u> W X <u>Y</u> Z.

The missing term is, therefore, P.

24. H. 100 – 3*n*

The variable n represents the position of the number in the set. When $n = 1$, the number must be 97. When $n = 2$, the number must be 94. When $n = 3$, the number must be 91.

When $n = 4$, the number must be 88. Try one or more of these values of n in the formulas provided as choices and note that you get the right answers with the formula $100 - 3n$.

25. B. 105

The average is the result of the division of the sum of all values by the number of values. There are four values, so we can write $420 \div 4 = 105$.

Lesson 3

1. D. 1 : 3
Assume that the width of the rectangle is x and the length is $2x$. We can find the perimeter in terms of x: $P = 2(x + 2x) = 6x$. The ratio of the length of the rectangle to its perimeter is $2x : 6x = 1 : 3$.

2. E. 25 : 9
Since $a : b = 3 : 5$, the ratio $b : a = 5 : 3$ and $10b : 6a = (10 \cdot 5) : (6 \cdot 3) = 50 : 18 = 25 : 9$.

3. D. 1 : 10
The best way to find the ratio is to multiply $\frac{a}{b}$ by $\frac{b}{c} : \frac{a}{b} \cdot \frac{b}{c} = \frac{1}{2} \cdot \frac{1}{5} = \frac{1}{10}$ or $1 : 10$.

4. F. 7 : 16
Since $1 : X = 7 : 2$, $X = 2/7$.
$X + 2 = 2 + 2/7 = 16/7$. $1 \div \frac{16}{7} = \frac{7}{16}$ or $7:16$.

5. D. 3 : 4
Let the side of the square be a and the side of the equilateral triangle be b. It is given that $4a = 3b$. Divide both sides of the equation by $4b$ and you will find the ratio $a : b = 3 : 4$.

6. H. 9
If 2 mangos cost as much as 1 pear, 4 mangos cost as much as 2 pears or as much as 9 apples.

7. D. 1.5 : 10
$15\% = 0.15$ or $15 : 100$ or $1.5 : 10$.

8. G. 10 : 11
Let's say the ratio of the number of boys to the number of girls is $b : g$. That means that there is some integer x, for which $bx + gx$ is equal to the total number of people, which is 42. We can write that sum as $x(b + g) = 42$, which means that $b + g$ must be a factor of 42. Among the choices, only the sum of $10 + 11 = 21$ is the factor of 42 and we can find the number of boys and girls by using the equation $10x + 11x = 42$.

9. C. 34.7
1.27% is one-tenth of 12.7%, so simply take one-tenth of 347 to get 34.7.

10. G. 32
You can reword the problem statement to say that there are $3x$ gray and $5x$ white mice in the cage, for a total is $8x$. If 3 more gray mice are added to the cage, there will be $(3x + 3) / (5x)$, which we are told is equal to 3/4.
Solving this equation, we get: $4(3x + 3) = 3(5x)$ or $12x + 12 = 15x$, $3x = 12$ and therefore $x = 4$.
Since there were originally $8x$ mice in the cage, the answer is $8x = 32$.

11. D. 48.5%
Assume that Sam got $v\%$ of the votes and Ben got $(v + 3)\%$ of the vote.
You can then write: $v + (v + 3) = 100$ or $2v + 3 = 100$, $2v = 97$, and therefore $v = 48.5\%$.

12. F. $150

Call the original price of the coat p. An increase of 20% can be written as $p + 0.2p = 1.2p$. The subsequent 20% decrease can be written as:
$1.2p - 0.2(1.2p) = 0.96p$.
Since $0.96p = 144$, $p = 144 \div 0.96 = 150$.

13. A. 24

$0.12 \cdot (1/2) \cdot 400 = 24$.

14. E. 1 : 32

Note that these are sequential powers of 2. Therefore, the 5th term is 2^5 and 10th term is 2^{10}. The ratio is $2^5 : 2^{10} = 1 : 2^5 = 1 : 32$.

15. D. 12 : 50

$24\% = 24 : 100 = 12 : 50$.

16. G. –2

The opposite of 0.5 is –0.5 and the reciprocal of (–0.5) is –2.

17. D. 1.5%

The actual interested earned is $1,218 – $1,200 = $18. $18 out of $1200 is $18/1200 = 0.015 = 1.5\%$.

18. F. 180

Let the larger number be x. That makes the other number $0.05x$. We are told that $x + 0.05x = 63$, which means $1.05x = 63$ and $x = 60$. 5% of 60 is 3 and therefore the product of the two numbers is $60 \cdot 3 = 180$.

19. B. 125%

Since the exact length of the radius doesn't matter, we can use any convenient number. Suppose the radius of the original circle is 2. Then, increasing it by 50% makes the radius 3.

The area of the original circle is 4π and the area of the new circle is 9π. The area increased by $9\pi - 4\pi = 5\pi$. The ratio of the amount of increase to the old area is $5\pi/4\pi$, or 1.25. Therefore, the percentage increase is 125%.

20. H. 35%

Let $m = 7x$ and $n = 13x$. The sum $(m + n) = 20x$. Find the ratio of m to $(m + n)$: $7x/20x = 7/20$ or 0.35 or 35%.

21. D. 50%

There is a total of 8 integers. Four of them, 2, 3, 5, and 7 are prime. That means that 1/2 or 50% are prime.

22. E. 12.5%

To find the number of multiples of 3 below 25, divide 25 by 3 and take the whole part of the answer. 25/3 = 8r1, which means there are 8 multiples of 3 that are smaller than 25. Of these, only 3 itself is a prime (all others are divisible by 3). One out of eight is $1/8 = 0.125 = 12.5\%$.

23. C. 1%

10% of 10% of N = $0.1 \cdot 0.1 \cdot N = 0.01N = 1\%$ of N.

24. E. 44%

Start with a convenient value for N: N = 100 (since it can correspond to 100%). Then calculate that 100 + 20% of 100 = 100 + 20 = 120, and 120 + 20% of 120 = 120 + 24 = 144. Finally, 144 – 100 = 44 which means that the total increase is 44%.

25. B. 9

The sum is 7 + 9 + 11 + 13 + 20 = 60. 15% of 60 is 6 + 3 = 9.

Lesson 4

1. A. 0.45

Write the problem statement as an equation: 0.1 in / 25 mi = x in / 112.5 mi. Use the cross multiplication to find x: (25 mi)(x in) = 11.25 mi · in, and x = 0.45 in.

2. E. 16 : 25

Let k be the ratio of the two cubes' edge lengths. The ratio of the volumes of the two cubes is the cube (3rd power) of the ratio of their edge lengths. Therefore, k^3 = 64/125 and k = 4/5. The ratio of their surface areas is the square (2nd power) of the ratio of their edge lengths, or k^2 = 16/25.

3. C. △△

The initial scale balance indicates that ○○ = △. Therefore, we can write △○○ as △△.

4. F. 14

The ratio of the areas is the square (second power) of the scale factor of the two triangles. Call the scale factor k and therefore k^2 = 49/81, or k = 7/9. Call the longest side of the smaller triangle L, and use the proportion $L/18$ = 7/9 to find the longest side of the small triangle: L = 14.

5. D. 0.01

Since 1 cm represents 10 m, 1 cm^2 = 1 cm · 1 cm will represent 10 m · 10 m = 100 m^2. In order to find how many square centimeters would represent 1 m^2, divide 1 cm^2 by 100 m^2 to get 0.01.

6. E. $\frac{60AC}{B}$

C minutes are equal to 60 · C seconds. Tim can do A / B pull-ups per 1 second, and therefore he can do: (A/B pullups/sec) · (60C sec/min) = (60AC)/B pullups / min, or $\frac{60AC}{B}$.

7. C. 81 cm²

The scale factor of similarity of the two rectangles is 18/12 = 3/2. Therefore, the ratio of the area of the second rectangle to the first is equal to $(3/2)^2$ = 9/4 and its area is 36 · (9/4) = 81 cm^2.

8. F. 25 yd²

The radius of the first circle is equal to the square root of 625 / π yd^2, which is 25 / $\sqrt{\pi}$ yd. The radius of the other circle is equal to one fifth of that, or 5 / $\sqrt{\pi}$ yd, and the area of the second circle is therefore π times $(5 / \sqrt{\pi})^2$ or 25 yd^2.

9. D. 7200

Since 1 yd = 3 ft, 6 feet = (6 ft ÷ 3 ft/yd) = 2 yd, and 6 ft/sec = 2 yd/sec, or 2 · 60 = 120 yd/min, or 120 · 60 = 7200 yd/hour.

10. E. 675 m²

Since on the scale drawing, the length is 3 times the width, the real field also has a length that is 3 times its width. The length is 45 m, so the width is 15m and the area is therefore 45 · 15 = 675 m^2.

11. C. 1 in : 15 m

The ratio of the dimensions of the real rectangle are 4 to 11, just like in the scale drawing. Call the length 11x and the width is 4x; you can then write the equation for the area as (11x)(4x) = 9900 m^2, or x^2 = 9900 / (4 · 11) = 225 m^2, which means that $x = 15$ m. Since in the scale drawing, the same value corresponds to 1 inch, the scale factor is 1 in : 15 m.

12. F. 5 : 1

The ratio of the areas of two circles is 25 : 1, which is the second power of the linear scale factor. Therefore, the linear scale factor (first power, or length scale factor, which corresponds to the radius scale factor) is 5 : 1.

13. D. 35 qt

20 qt is 5 times 4 qt, which means that you can make 5 times the amount of green paint than you can with 4 qt of yellow paint. Since you can make 7 qt of green paint with 4 qt of yellow paint, with 20 qt of yellow paint, you can make 7 qt $\cdot$ 5 = 35 qt of green paint.

14. E. 1 cm : 10 km

2 cm of the original map would be equivalent to 10 km, so 1 cm of the new map will also be equivalent to 10 km. Therefore, the new scale factor is 1 cm : 10 km.

15. A. 21%

Increase by 10% means 100% + 10% = 110% or a scale factor of 1.1.
The scale factor for areas will be equal to the second power of linear scale factor, which is $(1.1)^2 = 1.21$. Therefore, the area of the new play space will be equal to $1.21 \cdot (3 \cdot 5) = 18.5$. The area will increase by $18.15 - 15 = 3.15$.
3.15 out of 15 is $3.15/15 = 315/1500 = 21/100 = 21\%$.

16. E. 25%

In order to increase the area of the square from 16 in^2 to 25 in^2, we need to increase each side from 4 in to 5 in.
$5 - 4 = 1$. 1 in is 1/4 of 4 in, or 25%.

17. B. 0.05 m^2

100 dm^2 = 1 m^2 is given. If you divide both sides of the equation by 20, you will get 5 dm^2 = 1/20 m^2 or 0.05 m^2.

18. G. 1 in : 2 mi

If the scale factor of the areas is 0.25 in^2 : 1 mi^2, the scale factor of the line segments will be the square root of the areas ratio, which is 0.5 in : 1 mi, which is the same as 1 in : 2 mi.

19. C. $55.47

$129 \cdot \$0.43 = \$55.47$
A quick shortcut: use rounded values to make an estimate: $130 \cdot 0.4 \approx 52$, and pick the closest answer.

20. H. 800%

The linear scale factor of the two triangles is $12/4 = 3$. The area of the large triangle is $3^2 = 9$ times bigger than the area of the small one. So if the area of the small triangle is A, the area of the large one is $9A$. The difference between areas is $9A - A = 8A$. Since A is 100% of the area, 8A is 800%.

21. B. $2.80

$\$25.20 \div 9 = \$2.80$ per gallon.

22. G. 1 : 2

The scale factor of the two volumes is 12 : 96 = 1 : 8. Since the volumes are third degrees of the linear measures of the can and its model, in order to find the scale factor for the model, we should find the cubic root of 1/8, which is 1/2 or 1 : 2.

23. C. 1.6 in
24 miles is 8 times bigger than 3 miles, so the distance on the map will be 8 times bigger than 0.2 inches, or $0.2 \cdot 8 = 1.6$ in.

24. G. 4 : 1
The length of the mid-segment of the triangle is 1/2 of the base, and forms a smaller triangle that is similar to the original triangle. Since the linear scale factor is 1/2, the scale factor of their areas will be $(1/2)^2 = 1/4$. Thus, the ratio of the area of the original triangle to the area of the small one is 4 : 1.

25. D. 0.0025
$(0.1 \text{ in})^2 = (2 \text{ mi})^2$ or $0.01 \text{ in}^2 = 4 \text{ mi}^2$. Since 4 mi^2 is equivalent to 0.01 in^2, 1 mi^2 will be equivalent to $0.01 \text{ in}^2 \div 4 = 0.0025 \text{ in}^2$.

Lesson 5

1. C. 900°
If n is the number of sides of any polygon, the sum of all interior angles S(n) is equal to 180°(n − 2). The difference S(10) − S(5) = 180° · ((10 − 2) − (5 − 2)) or 180° · 5 or 900°.

2. E. 35°
The average is (180° − 110°) ÷ 2 = 35°.

3. B. 142°
The measure of any exterior angle of the triangle is equal to the sum of two remote interior angles, so the answer is 142°.

4. H. 75°
Assume that the measure of the smaller angle is x and the measure of the larger angle is $5x$. By definition of complementary angles, $x + 5x = 90°$, or $6x = 90°$, and $x = 15°$. The larger angle is there 5·15° = 75°.

5. C. 36°
Since the sum of all exterior angles of any polygon is 360°, the average of all exterior angles of the decagon is 360° ÷ 10 = 36°.

6. H. 24 in
Since the length of any side of the triangle must be less than the sum and larger than the difference of two other sides, 12 − 7 < AC < 12 + 7 or 5 < AC < 19. That means the third side must be larger than 5, and therefore the perimeter P must be larger than (5 + 7 + 12) = 24 and thus cannot be equal to 24 in.

7. D. 36°
Each interior angle of the regular pentagon is 180° · (5 − 2) = 108°. We have two symmetrical congruent isosceles triangles and one isosceles triangle with angle x we need to find. Angles of each of the two congruent triangles are 36°, 108° and 36°. Using the top angle of the pentagon, we can write $x + 2 · 36° = 108°$. Therefore, $x + 72° = 108°$, and $x = 36°$.

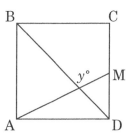

8. G. 36°
Call the two vertical angles (the angles formed by the intersection in the middle of the diagram) z, since vertical angles have the same measure. Since each triangles' three angles add up to 180°, we can write that $64° + 76° + z = 104° + x° + z$. Subtract z from both sides and simplify to get $x° = 36°$.

9. D. 103°

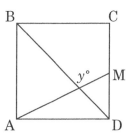

$y°$ is the vertical angle of the top angle of the triangle with base AD, which means it's equal to the top angle. The measure of the angle MAD is given to be 32° and the measure of ADB is 45° (BD is the diagonal of the square). Therefore, we can write: $y° = 180° − 45° − 32° = 103°$.

10. F. 120°

Each altitude of the equilateral triangle is the bisector of the interior 60° angle, which means that angles MNP and NMP are 30° each, and n = 180° − 30° − 30° = 120°.

11. D. 130°

When it's 8:20, the minute hand points at the 4 and the hour hand is between 8 and 9 on the 1/3 of the hour sector (20/60 = 1/3). Each hour sector is 30° on the clockface, and there are 4 hours between 4 and 8, and 1/3 of the hour between 8 and the hour hand. Therefore, the angle between hands is the sum of 4 equal 30° angles, and 1/3 of 30° = 10°. The total measure is 130°.

12. E. 0°

Any trapezoid is a quadrilateral with the sum of all four interior angles equal to 360°, which averages to 90°. Any angle of a rectangle is 90°, and therefore the difference is 90° − 90° = 0°.

13. C. 6π

Tangent CG is perpendicular to the diameter EF and triangle EFG is a special 30°–60°–90° triangle. That means that the leg opposite to the 30° angle is equal to one-half of the hypotenuse EG. Therefore, EF = 6. Since EF is the diameter of the circle, the circumference is equal to 6π.

14. G. 90°

Assume that the measure of the small angle is x and the measure of the larger is $3x$. By definition of complementary angles, $x + 3x = 180°$, or $4x = 180°$, and

$x = 45°$. The larger angle is $3 \cdot 45° = 135°$, and the difference is $135° − 45° = 90°$.

15. B. 8π

The measure of the angle CAB of a right isosceles triangle is 45°, which is 1/8th of the full circle of 360°. Therefore, the area of the sector will be equal to 1/8th of the area of the circle with radius 8 (since AC is equal to BC, and AC is the radius of the circle). The area of such a circle is 64π, and 64π ÷ 8 is 8π.

16. G. 86°

Since the sum of two exterior angles of the triangle is 266°, and the sum of all three exterior angles is 360°, the measure of the third exterior angle is 360° − 266° = 94°. One interior angle is supplementary to this exterior angle, and their sum is 180°, which means the interior angle is equal to 180° − 94° = 86°.

17. A. 19°

$x°$ is one of the interior angles of a small triangle with two given exterior angles measuring 106° and 93°. Since the sum of all external angles of a triangle is 360°, we can find the measure of the third exterior angle, which is supplementary to the angle $x°$: 360° − (106° + 93°) = 161°. $x° = 180° − 161° = 19°$.

18. H. 36°

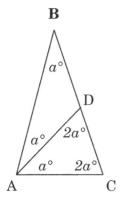

Since it is given that BD = AD, the measures of two angles ABD and BAD are the same and each is equal to $a°$. The exterior angle ADC of the triangle ABD is $2a°$. Since AC = AD, the measure of angle ACD is also $2a°$, AB = BC and the measure of angle BAC is also $2a°$. Now we have the triangle ADC with $a° + 2a° + 2a° = 180°$ and $a° = 36°$.

19. C. 33

The third side of the triangle must be less than $6 + 11 = 17$, so the largest integer value it can be is 16. Therefore, the largest possible integer perimeter value is $6 + 11 + 16 = 33$.

20. F. 113°

The angle between $a°$ and $b°$ is vertical with the angle that's equal to 67° and is therefore also equal to 67°. All three angles together make a straight angle, which means that $a° + b° + 67° = 180°$ or $a° + b° = 113°$.

21. D. 105°

Based on the given information, ABD and CBD are two special triangles: ABD is 45°–90°–45° and CBD is 30°–90°–60°. The measure of the angle ABC is, therefore, $45° + 60° = 105°$.

22. H. 133°

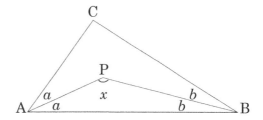

Draw the diagram and label the bisected angles A and B, calling them $2a$ and $2b$. Since angle C is 86°, for triangle ABC, we can write that $2a + 2b + 86° = 180$ or $2a + 2b = 94°$ or $a + b = 47°$. Then, for triangle APB, we can write that $a + b + x = 180°$, which means that the measure of angle APB is $180° - 47° = 133°$.

23. B. 79°

Connect two points B and D to get an isosceles triangle BCD. Since the base angles of an isosceles triangle are equal, the measure of angle BDC is equal $(180° - 112°) ÷ 2 = 34°$, and the measure of the angle ADC is equal to ADB + BDC $= 34° + 45° = 79°$.

24. H. 0

Side with length 12 must be larger than the magnitude of difference (nonnegative value) between the other two sides, and smaller than their sum. Therefore, the difference between the other two sides must be less than 12, and the smallest such value among the possible choices is 0.

25. B. Right

We can call the measures of the angles $4x$, $5x$, and $9x$ respectively, and write $4x + 5x + 9x = 180°$. That means $x = 10°$, and the angles of our triangle are 40°, 50°, and 90°, which makes this a right triangle.

Lesson 6

1. D. 24

1/4			

	1/3		

		6	6

6	6	6	6

Use a diagram like the one above to solve this problem. First, show four quarters and mark the 1/4th that was solved in the first 15 minutes. Then, note that there are 3/4ths of the total left, and one of these can be marked as 1/3rd. Finally, note that the remaining set has 12 problems, which means there were 24 problems to start with.

2. G. $51

Use the strategy of working backwards: Mrs. Wagner ended the day with $17. Before the second store, she had twice the money she ended the day with: $17 · 2 = $34. She had $34 after spending 1/3rd of her money in the first store, which means that $34 is 2/3rds of her original amount. $34 ÷ (2/3) = $51.

3. D. 3

The fact that the perimeter of the rectangle is 6 times its width can be written as P = 6W. The perimeter is twice the sum of the length and the width, so it can also be written as P = 2L + 2W = 6W. That means 2L = 4W or L = 2W. Therefore, the perimeter 6W is 3 · 2W = 3L, or 3 times as large as the length of the rectangle.

4. E. 0

If k is an even number, $(k + 2)$ is also an even number. A square of an even number must have a factor of $2^2 = 4$, which means that $(k + 2)^2$ is divisible by 4. Therefore, the remainder is 0.

5. C. 64 : 1

One hour consists of 6 ten-minute intervals. Call the initial number of bacteria a, and construct a table tracking the number of bacteria after every 10 minute interval:

Time (min)	Start	10	20	30	40	50	60
# of bacteria	a	$2a$	$4a$	$8a$	$16a$	$32a$	$64a$

The ratio is $64a \div a = 64 : 1$.

6. G. 979

The rule for the described pattern is to add 10 for the 2nd number, 2 · 10 for the 3rd one, and so on. That means for the nth number, one needs to add $(n - 1) \cdot 10$. Therefore, the 100th number will be $-11 + 99 \cdot 10 = 979$.

7. B. 36

The product of the first 50 prime numbers has only one factor of 2, and one factor of 3. Therefore, it cannot be divisible by 36, because $36 = 2 \cdot 2 \cdot 3 \cdot 3$.

8. G. 0.75

$A = \frac{1}{2} + \frac{1}{4} = \frac{3}{4} = 0.75$

9. D. 100

Because there are 10 odd numbers from 1 to 19, there are 10 parentheses-enclosed sums in the given expression. Because the signs alternate, when we expans all the parenthetical expressions, all t's will cancel out, and we will simply need to find the sum of all odd numbers from 1 to 19. Pair them up so that the sum of every pair is the same to get: $(1 + 19) + (3 + 17) + \ldots + (9 + 11) = 5 \cdot 20 = 100$.

10. E. –10

Since p and q can be either negative or positive, to minimize their difference, we should make q negative and p positive. Use $q = -9$ and $p = 1$ to get $(q - p) = -9 - 1 = -10$.

11. A. 3/2

Among provided answers, all fractions have a numerator that is 1 larger than the denominator. Fractions like that can be written as $(a + 1)/a$, which can be simplified to $1 + 1/a$. Therefore, the smaller the value of a, the larger the fraction (since $1/a$ gets bigger as a gets smaller). Thus, 3/2 is the largest fraction among provided choices.

12. E. 8

The numerator 6 is divisible by ± 1, ± 2, ± 3, and ± 6. Therefore, there are 8 possible values of N that produce an integer when 6 is divided by N.

13. B. 8

Assume that Steve started on floor F. Then you can write: $F + 7 - 8 + 3 = 10$. Solve the equation for F to get 8.

14. F. 13

If N is my favorite number, you can write the described operations as an equation: $(N - 7) \cdot 3 + 2 = 20$. Simplifying and solving: $(N - 7) \cdot 3 = 20 - 2$, which leads to $(N - 7) \cdot 3 = 18$, $(N - 7) = 6$, and finally $N = 13$.

15. C. 56 yards

Work backwards: Ann ended with 7 yards, and before that had twice that amount $(7 \cdot 2)$, and before that, twice that amount $(7 \cdot 2 \cdot 2)$, and before that, she started with twice that: $7 \cdot 2 \cdot 2 \cdot 2 = 56$.

16. H. 10

The easiest approach here is to write out all possible 3-digit numbers that satisfy the given condition, organizing them by the hundreds digit:

103	202	301	400
112	211	310	
121	220		
130			

3-digit numbers greater than 400 cannot have a digit sum of 4, since it will always be larger than 4.

17. B. 315

Find the prime factors of $1260 = 2 \cdot 2 \cdot 3 \cdot 3 \cdot 5 \cdot 7$. To compose the largest factor that is not divisible by 6, combine all the factors except 2s (2s are the smallest factors, and not having them will ensure that the product is not divisible by 6). The result is: $3 \cdot 3 \cdot 5 \cdot 7 = 315$.

18. F. 15

Write the given description as an equation: $(x / 5) = x - 12$. Multiply both sides by 5 to get $x = 5x - 60$ or $4x = 60$, or $x = 15$.

19. A. $10

If we call Jack's amount x dollars, then Kathy has $x + 13$ dollars and Vanessa has $x + 16$ dollars. Together, they have $x + x + 13 + x + 16 = 59$, or $3x + 29 = 59$ or $3x = 30$, or $x = 10$.

20. H. 19

Let there be x children and y adults in the group. We know that $x + y = 25$. We also know that $6x + 15y = 204$ ($6 per child, and $15 per adult adds up to $204). Multiple the first equation by 5, to get $5x + 5y = 125$, and divide the second equation by 3 to get $2x + 5y = 68$. Now subtract the second equation from the first one to get $3x = 57$, $x = 19$.

21. D. 2.5

Replace a with -2: $|-2| - 1 \div (-2) = 2 + 0.5 = 2.5$.

22. E. 38

Replace b with (-7) : $- (5 \cdot (-7) - 3) = -(-35 - 3) = 38$.

23. C. 15

Recall that $m^2 - n^2 = (m - n)(m + n)$. Also note that $-m-n = -(m + n)$. Then substitute given values to get: $(-3) \cdot (-5) = 15$.

24. E. 6

The area of a rectangle is length (L) times width (W). The new area will be $3L \cdot 2W = 6(L \cdot W)$, or 6 times bigger.

25. C. 48.8%

Pick a convenient initial cost for the coat, since it's not specified: $100. Then perform the reductions described in the problem: $100 minus 20% of $100 is $80; $80 minus 20% of $80 is $80 – $16 = $64, and finally, $64 minus 20% of $64 is $64 – $12.80 = $51.20. Thus, the total amount of reduction is $100 – $51.20 = $48.80, or 48.8 out of 100, which is 48.8%.

Lesson 7

1. **C.** $\frac{1}{6}$

The probability that the first marble will be red is $\frac{4}{9}$. Assuming the first marble is red (since we are asked to compute the probability of both marbles being red), the probability that the second marble will be red is $\frac{3}{8}$ (there are 3 red marbles left in the bag, and 8 marbles total). The probability that the first and the second both marble will be red is equal to the product of $\frac{4}{9} \cdot \frac{3}{8} = \frac{1}{6}$.

2. **H. 2000**

We have two letters for the first position, and 10 possible digits for each of the subsequent three positions to choose from. Using the Fundamental Counting Principle, the number of all possible codes is equal to $2 \cdot 10 \cdot 10 \cdot 10 = 2000$.

3. **C. 24**

There are four kids to choose from to place in seat 1, three kids for seat 2, and so on. Thus, the number of possible arrangements is $4 \cdot 3 \cdot 2 \cdot 1 = 24$.

4. **H. 3**

To get the smallest possible number of children who are guaranteed to have the same birthday month, assume that the birthdays are distributed evenly among all 12 months. Then, among 24 kids we would have exactly two students in each month, and since we have 25 students, there's one extra person with a birthday in one of the months. Therefore, the smallest possible number of students in

a class of 25 with the same birthday month is 3.

5. **A.** $\frac{1}{3}$

There are 6 possible ways of picking the cubes, and it helps to list them all: RBG, RGB, BRG, BGR, GBR, and GRB. Of these six, two have the red cube as last. Therefore, the probability is $\frac{2}{6} = \frac{1}{3}$.

6. **H.** $\frac{1}{9}$

The total area of the target is 9π. The area of the smallest circle is π. The probability of the dart hitting the center circle is $\pi \div 9\pi = 1/9$.

7. **A. 20**

All numbers between 30 and 39 have a digit 3, and 33 has two 3s, which gives us a total of 11 3s and one 7 in 37. Besides that, we have 3, 13, 23, 43, and 7, 17, 27, and 47 which gives us 4 more 3s and 4 more 7s. The total is $11 + 1 + 4 + 4 = 20$.

8. **G. 32**

$1568 = 2 \cdot 2 \cdot 2 \cdot 2 \cdot 2 \cdot 7 \cdot 7$. Therefore, the largest factor not divisible by 7 is $2 \cdot 2 \cdot 2 \cdot 2 \cdot 2 = 32$.

9. **B. 12**

Two boys can sit in the first and the last chairs in two different ways. Among the three remaining chairs, the three girls could sit in $3 \cdot 2 \cdot 1 = 6$ different ways. Thus, the total number of combinations is $2 \cdot 6 = 12$.

10. E. 125

There are 5 odd digits in all: 1, 3, 5, 7 and 9. Therefore, for a 3-digit number consisting entirely of odd digits, we have 5 picks for every position. Thus, we can make $5 \cdot 5 \cdot 5 = 125$ different 3-digit numbers with odd digits.

11. B. 3

Write out a few consecutive powers of 3: $3^1 = 3, 3^2 = 9, 3^3 = 27, 3^4 = 81, 3^5 = 243$. Notice that the ones digits are in a repeating pattern of four digits: 3, 9, 7, 1, 3, 9, 7, 1, … Therefore, in order to find the unit digit of the 3^{13}, we need to divide 13 by 4 and find the remainder, which is 1. Therefore, the first digit in the pattern of four digits will be the units digits – and the first digit is 3.

12. H. 128

$128 = 2^7$, which means that 128 has 7 prime factors.
All others have fewer than 7:
$143 = 11 \cdot 13$ (2 prime factors),
$140 = 2 \cdot 2 \cdot 5 \cdot 7$ (4 prime factors),
$130 = 2 \cdot 5 \cdot 13$ (3 prime factors), and
$132 = 2 \cdot 2 \cdot 3 \cdot 11$ (4 prime factors).

13. B. 2

The answer to the question is simply the number of prime numbers between 20 and 30. There are two such prime numbers: 23 and 29.

14.　　G. $\frac{2}{5}$

Prime-numbered balls are: 2, 3, 5, 7, 11, 13, 17, or 19. Thus, there are 8 of them in a bag of 20, and the probability is 8/20 or $\frac{2}{5}$.

15. C. $\frac{1}{6}$

On the first pick, there are 2 red marbles in the bag, and 4 marbles total. On the second pick, assuming the first marble picked was red, there's just 1 red marble in the bag, and 3 marbles total. Therefore, the probability of picking two red marbles is: $(\frac{2}{4}) \cdot (\frac{1}{3}) = \frac{1}{6}$.

16. G. 1

Among the 14 people, it is certain that at least 2 people will have their birthday at the same month, because if 12 people all have different birthday months, the 2 remaining people have to have their birthday in one of those months.

17. C. 3

Since $7 \div 3 = 2r1$, one can place two birds in each of the first two cages, but the third cage will have to have 3 birds.

18. F. $\frac{1}{6}$

$1/7 = 0.142857142857\ldots$ – which means that the last digit when the decimal is rounded can be 1, 4, 3, 9, 6, or 7. 3 is one of the total 6 possible cases and therefore the probability to get 3 is $\frac{1}{6}$.

19. D. $\frac{1}{11}$

The total number of letters in the word MATHEMATICS is 11, of which one is C, and 10 are not C. Therefore, the probability of non-C in the first pick is 10/11, and probability of C on the second pick is 1/10, for a total of: $P = \frac{10}{11} \cdot \frac{1}{10} = \frac{1}{11}$.

20. E. 20%

Draw a diagram and mark the overlapping groups and non-overlapping groups accordingly:

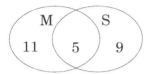

The total is 11 + 5 + 9 = 25, and the probability of having both As is 5 out of 25, or 20%.

21. B. $\frac{4}{5}$

There are 99 − 9 = 90 two-digit numbers. Among these, there are 9 numbers that end in 0 (10, 20, …, 90), and 9 numbers that end in 5 (15, 25,…, 95). Therefore, there are 9 · 2 = 18 are multiples of 5. That means 90 − 18 = 72 are not multiples of 5. Thus, the probability of picking a non-multiple of 5 is 72 ÷ 90 = 4/5.

22. G. $\frac{1}{24}$

The total number of all possible arrangements is 4 · 3 · 2 · 1 = 24. Of these, only one will form the word TALE. Therefore, the probability is $\frac{1}{24}$.

23. B. $\frac{2}{3}$

Since the area of the circle is 1/3 of the area of the square, the area outside of the circle but inside the square will be equal to 2/3^{rds} of the area of the square. Thus, the probability of selecting a point within it is $\frac{2}{3}$.

24. H. 12

Keep in mind that Mr. Jones is also part of the team. Therefore, there are 4 women and 3 men on the team. Every woman can end up in a group with any of the 3 men. Therefore, there are 4 · 3 = 12 possible groups.

25. C. $\frac{3}{16}$

There are 4 · 4 = 16 possible pairs of numbers. Among these, we can get a sum of 10 with 2 + 8, 7 + 3 or 9 + 1, which is 3 out of 16 possible pairs. Therefore, the probability of picking such a pair is $\frac{3}{16}$.

Lesson 8

1. D. $xy < 0$

For any point in the 4th quadrant, coordinates must be $x > 0$ and $y < 0$, which means that $xy < 0$.

2. E. 4

The reflection of A(–8 , –2) over x-axis is B(–8 , 2). Point A is 2 units above x-axis, and point B is 2 units below x-axis, which means that AB = 4.

3. D. 14

Let's use CD as the base of the triangle. The y-coordinates of C and D are the same, so the length of CD is simply the difference in x-coordinates, so CD = 7. Because the base of the triangle lies on the x-axis, the height of the triangle CDE is equal to the y-coordinate of E, which is 4. The area is, therefore, $(7 \cdot 4) \div 2 = 14$.

4. G. E(6, 0)

Since both point C and D are on the x-axis, we simply need to take the average of their x-coordinates to get the x-coordinate of point E. $(14 + (-2)) \div 2 = 6$, which means that E is at (6, 0).

5. B. Sign

Absolute value may change the sign of a number, if the number is negative.

6. H. Infinitely many

If we fix one of the vertices of a square at the origin and rotate the square, you will see that a square can be at an arbitrary angle. Because there are infinitely many values that angle can take, there are infinitely many such squares.

7. D. 4 units

If you take the steps described in the problem, you will have gone to points (4, 0), (4, 4), and (0, 4) – therefore, you'll end up 4 units away from the origin.

8. F. (–3 , 2)

All points on the line $x = -3$ have –3 as their x-coordinate, and all points on the line $y = 2$, have 2 as a y-coordinate. Therefore, the point at their intersection is (–3, 2).

9. A. 9 sq. units.

Use AC as the base of the triangle. The length of AC is 6, and the height of the triangle OB = 3. The area is therefore equal to $(6 \cdot 3) \div 2 = 9$.

10. G. (2, 2)

The first two points are a distance 3 away. Point (2, 3) is definitely further away from the origin than point (2, 2). The distance from point (2, 2) to the origin is $2\sqrt{2}$ or $\sqrt{8}$, which is less than 3, and therefore that's the point closest to the origin.

11. D. 8 sq. units

Since M and K are two opposite vertices, MK is the diagonal of the square and equal to 4. Using the Pythagorean theorem, you can deduce that each side of the square is therefore equal to $\sqrt{16/2} = \sqrt{8}$. Therefore, the area of the square is 8.

12. G. $cd > 0$

For any point in the 3rd quadrant, coordinates must be: $c < 0$ and $d < 0$, which means $cd > 0$.

13. D. 5

The midpoint of AB is M(–2,0). The midpoint of BC is N(3,0). Since both points are on the x-axis, the distance between them is the difference between their x-coordinates: MN = 3 – (–2) = 5.

14. H. Square

The square is exactly 2 units from the origin, but all other figures are further.

15. B. Star and Square

Both the star and the square are 2 units away from one axis, and 1 unit away from the other – that means they are the same distance away from the origin.

16. G. (2, 2)

Use the distance formula (you can also use a picture and the Pythagorean Theorem). $(2 - (-1))^2 + (2 - (-2))^2 = 9 + 16 = 25$. The distance is $\sqrt{25} = 5$.

17. B. 4π

The center of the circle is 2 units from the y-axis, and since the y-axis is the tangent of the circle, its radius (distance from the center of the circle to the tangent point) is 2. Therefore, the area of the circle is 4π.

18. E. 4

The distance between the center of the circle to any point on its circumference is the radius of the circle. Since points (4, –2) and (4, 0) have the same x-coordinate, the distance between them is

the difference between their y-coordinates. Therefore, the circle's radius is 2, and its diameter is 4.

19. B. 96

Based on the given information, the origin is the center of the rhombus and the vertex of a right triangle that constitutes one quarter of the rhombus. The hypotenuse of this triangle is 10 (the side of the rhombus) and one of the legs is 8. Using the Pythagorean Theorem, you can find the other leg, which is 6. That makes the area of this triangle (8 · 6) / 2 = 24. Since that's a quarter of the rhombus' area, the area of the entire figure is 24 · 4 = 96.

20. E. (0, –1)

(0, –1) is 1 unit from the x-axis, but all other points are further.

21. C. 12

The sides of the given right triangle are the Pythagorean triple 3, 4, 5 and the perimeter is equal to 3 + 4 + 5 = 12.

22. F. 10

This point is 6 units from the y-axis and 8 units from the x-axis. The given point, along with the origin and one of the points on the axes form a right triangle whose sides are a Pythagorean triple 6, 8, 10. The hypotenuse of the triangle is also the distance between the given point and the origin, and therefore the answer is 10.

23. C. $y + x = 4$

Line $y = x$ has a slope of 1, and so do lines in three of the four answers, but line $y + x = 4$ can be written as $y = -x + 4$, which makes it apparent that its slope is –1, and therefore it cannot be parallel to the given line.

24. G. 8

As shown on the diagram, the triangle is right, and its 4 units each. Its area is, therefore,

$(4 \cdot 4) \div 2 = 8$.

25. C. II or IV quadrant

It is given that $xy < 0$. That implies that either $x < 0$ and $y > 0$ (which puts the point in the IInd quadrant), or that $x > 0$ and $y < 0$, which puts the point in the IVth quadrant.

SHSAT MATH PRACTICE TEST

Suggested Time — 90 Minutes

57 QUESTIONS

Grid-In Problems

Questions 58 – 62

58.

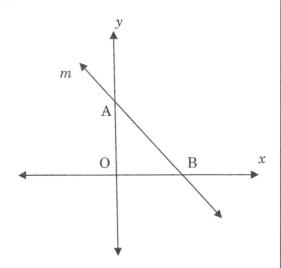

The equation of line m is $y = -x + 3$.

Find the area of triangle OAB.

59. How many prime numbers smaller than 100 have 1 as a units digit?

60. If the average of n, –5, and 2 equals to 7, what is n?

61. If $3x = 4y = 0.5z = -12$, what is the sum of $x + y + z$?

62. Sam paid $6.54 for 3 notebooks and 3 pens. How much will Sam's friend Jen pay if she bought 2 of the same kind of notebooks and 2 of the same kind of pens?

63. If the sum $ab + b + c$ is an even number, c is odd, and a is even, which of the following could be the value of b?

    A. 2

    B. 3

    C. 4

    D. 6

64. What number is 8 less than 5 times itself?

    E. 10

    F. 7

    G. 5

    H. 2

65. 15% of all marbles in the box are red, and 20% of all red marbles have a small hole. What percent of all marbles in the box are red and have a small hole?

    A. 3%

    B. 5%

    C. 25%

    D. 35%

66. Ann needs $\frac{2}{3}$ meters of fabric for a scarf. Which of the following lengths of fabric can be cut to the required length with the least amount of waste?

    E. $\frac{7}{8}$

    F. $\frac{8}{9}$

    G. $\frac{4}{5}$

    H. $\frac{5}{7}$

67. The operation ✕ is defined for all nonzero numbers by $t ✕ k = t^2 - (-k)$. Find $((-2) ✕ (-1)) ✕ 1$.

    A. 4

    B. 7

    C. 10

    D. 12

68. $\frac{2}{9}$ of all students in the class have blue eyes, and 21 students have another eye color. How many students are in the class?

E. 36

F. 27

G. 25

H. 22

69. The smallest of four positive consecutive integers is 4 times smaller than the largest. What is the sum of all four integers?

A. 13

B. 11

C. 10

D. 7

70. If $\frac{a+2b}{b} = \frac{7}{2}$, what is the ratio of a to b?

E. $\frac{1}{2}$

F. $\frac{3}{2}$

G. $\frac{5}{2}$

H. $\frac{3}{7}$

71. $4h^2 - k = k + 1$. Express k in terms of h.

A. $2h^2 - 0.5$

B. $4h^2 - 1$

C. $4h^2 + 1$

D. $2h^2 + 0.5$

72. ABCDE is a regular pentagon. Find the measure of angle DEB.

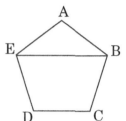

E. 86°

F. 84°

G. 72°

H. 36°

73. If P is an odd number, how many even numbers are between P – 3 and P + 3, exclusive of these values?

A. 1

B. 2

C. 3

D. 4

74. The product of 4 consecutive even integers is 0. Among the choices below, what is the smallest possible value for one of these integers?

E. −8
F. −6
G. −4
H. −2

75. Solve for y: $15y - 11 = 2 - 11y$.

A. 2
B. 0.5
C. 2.25
D. 3.25

76. If m and n are positive integers and $(mn + n)$ is an odd integer, which of the following must be true?

E. n is odd and m is even.
F. n is even and m is even.
G. n is odd and m is odd.
H. n is even and m is odd.

77. If $a + b + c = 20$, $a + b + 2c = 29$, and $a + 2b + c = 27$, what is a?

A. 7
B. 6
C. 5
D. 4

78.

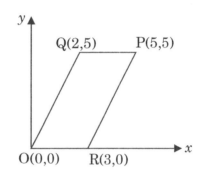

What is the area of the parallelogram QPRO?

E. 17
F. 15
G. 12
H. 7.5

79. Carlo's salary changed from $15 per hour to $18 per hour. What percent did it change by?

A. 20%
B. 15%
C. 5%
D. 3%

80. Two point on the number line have coordinates H(–10.3) and P(14.7). If the line segment HP is divided into 2 congruent parts by a point M, what are its coordinates?

E. M(–4.3)

F. M(2.2)

G. M(4.7)

H. M(4.8)

81.

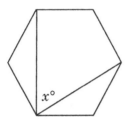

Find the measure of the acute angle $x°$ between two diagonals of a regular hexagon.

A. 18°

B. 36°

C. 48°

D. 60°

82. A car needs A gallons of gasoline to travel M miles. How many gallons of gasoline does this car need to travel N miles?

E. $\dfrac{AN}{M}$

F. $\dfrac{AM}{N}$

G. $\dfrac{M}{AN}$

H. $\dfrac{N}{MA}$

83. Solve for y: $0.5y = 5 + 0.3y$.

A. 50

B. 25

C. 5

D. 2.5

84. David wanted to keep an average speed of 12 mph in a bicycle race. However, he was only able to average 11 mph, and the race took 10 minutes longer than he planned. How long was the race in miles?

E. 1320 mi

F. 132 mi

G. 22 mi

H. 11 mi

85. What is the base of a triangle whose height is 8 cm and whose area is 32 cm²?

A. 32 cm

B. 16 cm

C. 8 cm

D. 4 cm

86.

Number of pencils	1	2	3	4	5	6	8
Number of students	2	6	7	4	5	6	2

There are 32 students in the class. The frequency table above shows the number of students who have 1, 2, 3, 4, 5, 6, or 8 pencils in their respective pencil boxes. What is the average number of pencils in all of the students' pencil boxes?

E. 3.6

F. 4

G. 4.2

H. 4.4

87. There are about 1.6 km in 1 mile. About how many miles are in 10 km?

A. 6.25 mi

B. 6 mi

C. 5.5 mi

D. 16 mi

88. What is the largest odd factor of 546?

E. 13

F. 91

G. 273

H. 279

89. If $3a - 2b = 17$ and $2a - 3b = 1$, what is $a + b$?

A. 15

B. 16

C. 17

D. 16.3

90. The perimeter of triangle ABC is 30 in. AB : BC : AC = 3 : 5 : 7. What is the length of the largest side of the triangle?

    E. 21 in
    F. 14 in
    G. 10 in
    H. 12 in

91. If $7 - 10^x = 6.998 + 10^x$, find x.

    A. −3
    B. −2
    C. −2
    D. 1

92. The largest of 6 consecutive integers is T. What is the mean (average) of all 6 integers in terms of T?

    E. $\frac{2T - 5}{2}$
    F. $\frac{2T + 5}{2}$
    G. $\frac{T + 2}{6}$
    H. $\frac{T}{6}$

93. 20 pencils (10 red and 10 blue) were randomly distributed among 5 boxes, so that there are 4 pencils in each box. What is the smallest number of boxes that must have at least 2 red pencils?

    A. 1
    B. 2
    C. 3
    D. cannot be determined

94. If $a = 37$ and $b = 63$, what is the value of $b^2 - a^2$?

    E. 250
    F. 260
    G. 2500
    H. 2600

95. Consider the following problem: "A fuel tank has Z gallons of gas. If you add 3 gallons, the tank will be $\frac{3}{4}$ full. If you then add 2 more gallons, the tank will be $\frac{4}{5}$ full. What is the capacity of the fuel tank?" Which of the values provided in the problem is not needed to solve it?

    A. 3 gallons
    B. $\frac{3}{4}$ full
    C. 2 gallons
    D. $\frac{4}{5}$ full

96. How many distinct prime factors does 98 have?

    E. 2

    F. 3

    G. 4

    H. 7

97.

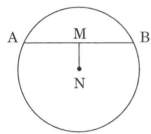

The center of the circle at point N is 3 cm from the chord AB. If the length of the chord AB is 8 cm, what is the area of the circle?

    A. 9π

    B. 16π

    C. 25π

    D. cannot be determined

98. Simplify: $2(4 - 3a) - 3(7 - 2a) =$

    E. -13

    F. $-13 - 6a$

    G. $6a - 13$

    H. 13

99. There are 6 blue and 10 white marbles in the box. What is the probability that the first 3 marbles randomly picked from the box will all be white?

    A. $\frac{3}{4}$

    B. $\frac{4}{5}$

    C. $\frac{3}{14}$

    D. $\frac{4}{15}$

100. A 2 in by 3 in rectangle was cut out from the corner of an 8 in by 6 in rectangle. Find the perimeter of the new figure.

    E. 22 in

    F. 23 in

    G. 24 in

    H. 28 in

101.

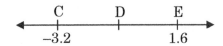

$$-3.2 \qquad 1.6$$

Point D is the midpoint of the line segment CE on the number line. What is the coordinate of the point D?

A. $-\dfrac{2}{4}$

B. $-\dfrac{4}{5}$

C. $\dfrac{3}{5}$

D. $\dfrac{4}{5}$

---

102. Suppose that m and n are integers and $-1 \leqslant m \leqslant 2$ and $-2 \leqslant n \leqslant 7$. What is the smallest possible value of mn?

E. -14

F. -7

G. 2

H. 4

103. All 32 students in a class took the Science test. 11 boys got a score that was less than or equal to 85, and 6 girls got a score greater than 85. How many boys received a score greater than 85, if 19 students got a score less or equal than 85?

A. 19

B. 13

C. 7

D. 6

---

104. A particular integer is odd and is a multiple of 3. Another integer is odd and is a multiple of 5. What is the possible sum of these integers?

E. 21

F. 22

G. 23

H. 24

105. If a teacher gives each student one notebook, he will have 5 notebooks left over. If he wants to give each student 2 notebooks, he will need 7 more notebooks. How many students are in the class?

A. 18
B. 16
C. 14
D. 12

106. P : T = 3 and T : K = 4. What is K : P?

E. 2 : 1
F. 3 : 4
G. 1 : 12
H. 7 : 12

107. Express the product of $(22 \times 10^3)(5 \times 10^2)$ in scientific notation form.

A. 1.1×10^5
B. 1.1×10^6
C. 1.1×10^7
D. 11×10^5

108. How many integers x satisfy the inequality $1 < 1 - 2x < 13$?

E. 7
F. 6
G. 5
H. 4

109. How many integers between –5 and 25 inclusive are divisible by 3, but not divisible by 12?

A. 3
B. 5
C. 6
D. 7

110. 7 integers have an average of 11. When one of the integers is removed, the new average becomes equal to 10. What integer was removed?

E. 7
F. 11
G. 13
H. 17

111. Two identical circles with radius 2 share one common point on their circumferences. What is the area of the smallest rectangle that can cover both circles?

    A. 16
    B. 24
    C. 30
    D. 32

112. Consider the string of letters: aoprtaoprtaoprtao…
If the same pattern continues, what will be the 50th letter?

    E. a
    F. o
    G. r
    H. t

113. How many 4-digit numbers can be written using digits 0, 1, and 3 if we can use the same digit as many times as we want?

    A. 56
    B. 54
    C. 27
    D. 18

114. The Sunrise Junior High School asked students to rank their favorite subjects (1st being their favorite, and 3rd – least favorite). The following table shows the three rankings students provided and how many students voted for each ranking.

	Ranking 1	Ranking 2	Ranking 3
1st	Math	Science	English
2nd	English	Math	Science
3rd	Science	English	Math
Votes	36	33	27

How many more students are there who prefer Math to English than there are students who prefer English to Math?

    E. 24
    F. 27
    G. 42
    H. 69

SHSAT Practice Test Answers

58.	4.5	87.	A
59.	5	88.	G
60.	24	89.	B
61.	–31	90.	F
62.	4.36	91.	A
63.	B	92.	E
64.	H	93.	B
65.	A	94.	H
66.	H	95.	A
67.	C	96.	E
68.	F	97.	C
69.	C	98.	E
70.	F	99.	C
71.	A	100.	H
72.	G	101.	B
73.	B	102.	F
74.	F	103.	C
75.	B	104.	H
76.	E	105.	D
77.	D	106.	G
78.	F	107.	C
79.	A	108.	G
80.	F	109.	D
81.	D	110.	H
82.	E	111.	D
83.	B	112.	H
84.	G	113.	B
85.	C	114.	G
86.	F		

SHSAT Practice Test Solutions

58. 4.5

Using the equation of the line, determine the coordinates of the points where it intersects the axes: A(0,3), and B(3,0). That means OA = 3 and OB = 3. Since the coordinate axes are perpendicular, the area of the triangle OAB is equal to (1/2)(3)(3) = **4.5.**

59. 5

1 is not prime, because the smallest prime is 2. 21, 51, and 81 are divisible by 3 and other factors; 91 is divisible by 7 and 13. Therefore, only 11, 31, 41, 61, and 71 are prime integers less than 100 with the units digit 1.

60. 24

$(n + (-5) + 2) \div 3 = 7$, $(n - 3) \div 3 = 7$, $n - 3 = 21$, and $n = $ **24.**

61. –31

$3x = -12 \rightarrow x = -4$; $4y = -12 \rightarrow y = -3$; $0.5z = -12 \rightarrow z = -24$. Therefore, $x + y + z = (-4) + (-3) + (-24) = $ **–31.**

62. 4.36

$\$6.54 \div 3 = \$2.18$ is the price of one notebook and one pen. Therefore, the price of 2 notebooks and 2 pens will be $\$2.18 \cdot 2 = $ **\$4.36.**

63. B.

$ab + b + c = b(a + 1) + c$ is even and c is odd (given). That means that the product $b(a + 1)$ must be odd (in order for its sum with c to be even). A product is odd only if each factor is an odd number. Therefore, b must be odd and the answer is $b = 3$.

64. H.

Let's call the unknown number x and write the problem statement as an equation: $5x - 8 = x$. Subtract x from both sides and add 8 to both sides to solve for $x = 2$.

65. A.

15% of 20% of any number N is $0.15 \cdot 0.2N = 0.03N$, which is 3% of the number.

66. H.

Find the difference between each answer and the provided quantity:

$$\frac{7}{8} - \frac{2}{3} = \frac{5}{24}$$
$$\frac{8}{9} - \frac{2}{3} = \frac{2}{9}$$
$$\frac{4}{5} - \frac{2}{3} = \frac{2}{15}$$
$$\frac{5}{7} - \frac{2}{3} = \frac{1}{21}$$

Note that among these answers, $\frac{1}{21}$ is the smallest.

67. C.

Simplify: $t \divideontimes k = t^2 - (-k) = t^2 + k$ to make the computation easier:

$(-2)^2 + (-1) = 4 - 1 = 3$, $3^2 + 1 = 10$.

68. F.

$1 - \frac{2}{9} = \frac{7}{9}$, which means that $\frac{7}{9}$ of all students is 21 or $\frac{7}{9} N = 21$, and

$N = 27$.

69. C.

Let's call the set of 4 consecutive integers: x, $x + 1$, $x + 2$, and $x + 3$. We are given that $x = (x + 3) \div 4$ or $x + 3 = 4x$. Solve for x to get $x = 1$. The sum is $1 + 2 + 3 + 4 = 10$.

70. F.

Split up the fraction and simplify:
$\frac{a+2b}{b} = \frac{a}{b} + \frac{2b}{b} = \frac{a}{b} + 2 = \frac{7}{2}$. Therefore, $\frac{a}{b} = \frac{7}{2} - 2 = \frac{3}{2}$.

71. A.

$4h^2 - k = k + 1$. Add k and subtract 1 from both sides to get: $4h^2 - 1 = k + k$, $2k = 4h^2 - 1$, and $k = 2h^2 - 0.5$.

72. G.

Each angle of a regular pentagon is equal to $180° \cdot (5 - 2) \div 5 = 108°$. Angle DEB is one of the angles of quadrilateral DEBC, and it's equal to angle EBC. The sum of all angles of quadrilateral DEBC is 360°, and since the angles D and C are

also both angles of the pentagon and equal to 108°, the sum of DEB and EBC is

$(360° - 2 \cdot 108°) = 144°$. Divide that by two to get the measure of angle DEB = 72°.

73. B.

Take any odd integer, for example P = 7 (for example) and use $7 - 3 = 4$ and $7 + 3 = 10$. 6 and 8 are the two even numbers between 4 and 10.

74. F.

If a product is equal to 0, one of the factors must be equal to 0. To minimize the first integer, 0 should be the largest even factor. That makes our product: $(-6)(-4)(-2)(0) = 0$. The smallest factor is, therefore, -6.

75. B.

Add $11y$ to both sides of the equation to get $26y - 11 = 2$. Then add 11 to both sides of the equation to get $26y = 13$, or $y = 13/26$ or 0.5.

76. E.

Since m and n are positive integers and $(mn + n)$ is an odd integer, use the inverse of the distributive property to rewrite the product as $n(m + 1)$. $n(m + 1)$ is odd, which means that both of its factors, n and $(m + 1)$, must also be odd. Therefore, n is odd, but m is even (1 less than the odd number $m + 1$).

77. D.

Subtract the first equation from the second to get $c = 9$, and then the first from the third, to get $b = 7$. Then replace c and b with 9 and 7 in the first equation to find
$a = 4$.

78. F.

The base of the parallelogram OR = 3 and its height is 5, because QP is 5 units above the base. Therefore, the area of the parallelogram is $3 \cdot 5 = 15$.

79. A.

The change in Carlo's salary is $18 − $15 = $3. $3 out of the original $15 is 1/5 or 0.2 = 20%.

80. F.

The easiest way to find the midpoint is to find the average of the two endpoint coordinates, which is $(−10.3 + 14.7) \div 2 = 2.2$.

81. D.

Connect two points to form a triangle. Note that each side of the triangle connects symmetric points of the hexagon, which means all three sides of the triangle are equal and it is equilateral. Therefore, $x = 60°$.

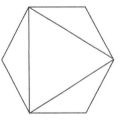

82. E.

Write the problem statement as a proportion: $\frac{A}{M} = \frac{X}{N}$, where X is the number of gallons needed to traven N miles. Then, use cross-multiplication to find X: $X = \frac{AN}{M}$.

83. B.

Subtract $0.3y$ from the both sides of the equation to get $0.2y = 5$, then divide both sides by 0.2 to get $y = 25$.

84. G.

Suppose David wanted to spend x hours for this race. Since the race took 10 minutes more, that means that he spent $(x + 1/6)$ hours, because 10 minutes = 1/6 hour. Since the length of the race can be represented both as the expected average speed times the expected time, and the actual average speed times the actual time, we can put these quantities in an equation: $12x = 11(x+1/6)$, or $12x = 11x + 11/6$, and finally $x = 11/6$ hrs. The length of the race is $12x = 12 \cdot (11/6) = 22$ mi.

85. C.

Since the area of the triangle is $(1/2) \cdot b \cdot h = 32$ (given), $b \cdot h = 64$. The height is 8, so $8b = 64$ and $b = 8$.

86. F.

Number of pencils	1	2	3	4	5	6	8
Number of students	2	6	7	4	5	6	2

In order to find the total number of pencils in the class, we should find the sum of the products: $1 \cdot 2 + 2 \cdot 6 + 3 \cdot 7 + 4 \cdot 4 + 5 \cdot 5 + 6 \cdot 6 + 8 \cdot 2 = 128$. The average number of pencils in each box is the total number of pencils divided by the total number of students, which is equal to $2 + 6 + 7 + 4 + 5 + 6 + 2 = 32$. $128 \div 32 = 4$.

87. A.

1 mile : 1.6 km = X miles : 10 km, or $\frac{1}{1.6} = \frac{X}{10}$. Use cross-multiplication to get: X = 10 ÷ 1.6 = 6.25.

88. G.

In order to find the largest odd factor of 546, divide 546 by 2 as many times as you can until you get an odd result, which would be largest odd factor: 546 ÷ 2 = 273, and 273 is odd, which makes it the largest odd factor.

89. B.

Subtract equation $2a - 3b = 1$ from $3a - 2b = 17$ → $(3a - 2b) - (2a - 3b) = 17 - 1$ → $3a - 2b - 2a + 3b = 16$ → $a + b = 16$.

90. F.

The perimeter of triangle ABC is 30 in, and AB : BC : AC = 3 : 5 : 7. We can therefore write the equation: $3x + 5x + 7x = 30$, and determine that $15x = 30$ and $x = 2$. The largest side is thus $7x = 7 \cdot 2 = 14$ in.

91. A.

To find x, add 10^x to both sides of the equation and subtract 6.998:

$7 - 6.998 = 2 \cdot 10^x$, or $0.002 = 2 \cdot 10^x$.

Divide both sides by 2, to get $10^x = 0.001$, and $x = -3$.

92. A.

Since the largest of 6 consecutive integers is T, the smallest is T – 5, and the mean (average) of all 6 integers in terms of T is equal to the average of these two terms:
$(T + T - 5) \div 2 = \frac{2T - 5}{2}$.

93. B.

To minimize the number of boxes with at least 2 red pencils, first distribute one red pencil to each box – this reduces the number of red pencils you have, but doesn't increase the number of boxes with 2 or more red pencils. You now have 5 pencils left: distribute them to maximize the number of red pencils in each box. Therefore, you would put 3 of the remaining pencils in one box, and 2 of the remaining pencils in another, creating 2 boxes with more than 2 pencils in each. That's an absolute smallest number of such boxes there can be.

94. H.

Since $b^2 - a^2 = (b - a)(b + a)$, $b^2 - a^2 = (63 - 37)(63 + 37) = 26 \cdot 100 = 2600$.

95. A.

In order to find the capacity of the tank, we need to consider that when it's at $\frac{3}{4}$ of its capacity and 2 gallons are added to it, it becomes $\frac{4}{5}$ full (the difference between $\frac{4}{5}$ and $\frac{3}{4}$ is equivalent to 2 gallons, and you would then divide 2 gallons by that value to find the capacity). That means that we don't need the 3 gallons value.

96. E.

$98 = 2 \cdot 7 \cdot 7$, which means there are 2 distinct prime factors: 2 and 7.

97. C.

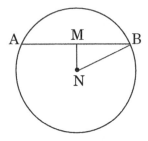

Center N of the circle is 3 cm from the chord AB, which means that MN = 3.

Since the length of the chord AB is 8 cm, BM = AM = 4 cm. For the right triangle NMB: $NB^2 = NM^2 + MB^2 = 3^2 + 4^2 = 25$. NB is the radius of the circle, and since the area of the circle is πr^2, it's equal to 25π.

98. E.

$2(4 - 3a) - 3(7 - 2a) =$
$8 - 6a - 21 + 6a = -13$.

99. C.

The probability for the first marble taken randomly to be white is $\frac{10}{16}$, for the second it's $\frac{9}{15}$, and for the third, it's $\frac{8}{14}$. Therefore, the probability for all three marbles taken randomly to be white is $\frac{10}{16} \cdot \frac{9}{15} \cdot \frac{8}{14} = \frac{3}{14}$.

100. H.

A rectangular shape cut from a corner of a larger rectangular shape does not change the perimeter of the larger shape (think of it as taking the two line segments in the corner and "pushing" them in – the total length of the perimeter won't change). Therefore, P = $2(6 + 8) = 28$ in.

101. B.

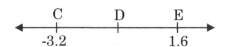

The best way to find the coordinate of the midpoint on the number line is to find the average of the endpoints of the segment, –3.2 and 1.6, which is $(–3.2 + 1.6) \div 2 = –0.8$ or $-\frac{4}{5}$.

102. F.

In order to minimize the product, we need to select the smallest possible factors. But since each factor can be negative, we should take the largest $n = 7$ and the smallest $m = –1$, to get the smallest possible product $mn = –7$.

103. C.

Let's make a table to visualize provided information:

	Score > 85	Score ≤ 85	Total
Girls	6		
Boys	?		11
Total		19	32

Now we can fill out the table just by using subtraction from the total:

	Score > 85	Score ≤ 85	Total
Girls	6		21
Boys	?		11
Total	13	19	32

Then:

	Score > 85	Score ≤ 85	Total
Girls	6	15	21
Boys	**7**	4	11
Total	13	19	32

Therefore, the answer is 7.

104. H.

Since the sum of two odd numbers is even, the possible answers are 22 or 24. Odd multiples of 5 less than 24 are 5 or 15.

$22 – 5 = 17$ and $24 – 5 = 19$ neither of which is a multiple of 3.

$22 – 15 = 7$ and $\mathbf{24} – 15 = 9$, and of these, only 9 is a multiple of 3. Therefore, the answer is 24.

105. D.

Call the number of notebooks that the teacher has N, and the number of students x. The first statement in the problem tells us that $N = x + 5$. The second statement tells is that $2x = N + 7$, or $N = 2x – 7$. Setting these values equal to each other, we get $1x + 5 = 2x – 7$. Solve for x to get $x = 12$.

106. G.

$\frac{P}{T} \cdot \frac{T}{K} = \frac{3}{1} \cdot \frac{4}{1} = 12$, and $\frac{P}{K} = 12$ or $\frac{K}{P} = \frac{1}{12}$.

107. C.

Use the commutative property of multiplication to rewrite:

$(22 \times 10^3)(5 \times 10^2) = (22 \times 5 \times 10^3 \times 10^2)$
$= 110 \times 10^5 = 1.1 \times 10^7$.

108. G.

First subtract 1 from each side of the inequality $1 < 1 - 2x < 13$ to arrive at $0 < -2x < 12$.

Now divide all 3 sides of the inequality by -2 (do not forget to switch the direction of the inequality, since you are dividing by a negative number): $-6 < x < 0$.

There are 5 integers $\{-5, -4, -3, -2, -1\}$ that satisfy this inequality.

109. D.

The question can be restated as asking us to find all multiples of 3 which are not divisible by 4 and are between -5 and 25 inclusive. We can list these integers: $-3, 3, 6, 9, 15, 18,$ and 21. The total are 7 integers.

110. H.

7 integers have an average of 11, which means that their sum is $7 \cdot 11 = 77$. When one of the integers is removed, the new sum will be $6 \cdot 10 = 60$. Since $77 - 60$ is 17, the removed integer is 17.

111. D.

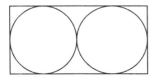

By drawing the diagram of the figure described in the problem, you can observe that the length of the rectangle is equal to 4r and the width of the rectangle is equal to 2r, where r is the radius of the circle.

$L = 4 \cdot 2 = 8$; $W = 2 \cdot 2 = 4$, and the area is $8 \cdot 4 = 32$.

112. H.

Since the group of 5 letters "aoprt" is repeating, and $50 \div 5 = 10$ with remainder 0, the 50th letter will be the same as the 5th letter, which is **t**.

113. B.

A 4-digit number has 4 spots for its digits. Since 0 cannot be in the first position, only two digits, 1 and 3, can occupy it. Any of the other three positions can be occupied by any of the three digits. Therefore, the total number of possible combinations is $2 \cdot 3 \cdot 3 \cdot 3 = 54$.

114. G.

Let's examine the table:

	Ranking 1	Ranking 2	Ranking 3
1st	Math	Science	English
2nd	English	Math	Science
3rd	Science	English	Math
Votes	36	33	27

36 students who voted for Ranking 1 and 33 students who voted for Ranking 2 prefer Math to English, but 27 students who voted for Ranking 3 prefer English to Math. $(36 + 33) - 27 = 42$.